By the Same Author

Breaking Freedom

Crossing Borders By Will Carr (as told to George)

Common Sense Series
You Are Going To Die (And That's Okay)
The Myth of Normal (Does anyone believe there is such a thing?)

Upcoming Titles in the Common Sense Series:
You Are *Creative (It's time to start reaping the benefits)*

Hearth Chronicles
A Thousand Reasons
Hearth I: Discovery
Hearth II: Home

Upcoming Titles in the Hearth Chronicles
Young at Hearth
A Sweet, Dark Quest

The Myth of Normal

(Does anyone believe there is such a thing?)

R.L. George

Hearth
2019

The Myth of Normal (Does anyone believe there is such a thing?)
Copyright © 2019 by R. L. George
Arizona, USA
author-rlgeorge.com
All rights reserved
ISBN: 9781672379342

This is not a scientific treatise; the ideas and suggestions in this book are not intended as professional advice, but are based on and speak to intuition and common sense.

All trademarks are the property of the author. Unauthorized reproduction or distribution of this copyrighted work is illegal. No part of this book may be used or reproduced except in the case of cited quotations in critical articles, reviews, or academic essays.

FIRST EDITION

For Pinkie Paranya
Dear Friend
Talented Author
Emphatic Normality Resister

Acknowledgments

Special thanks to the friends who help to keep me on track: Carrie and Gabe Negrete, Kelly and Philip Gladney, Kaysha Riggs, Brent Fetters, Jodi Weisberg, Monica Engle, Red Ortiz, Dee Strickland Johnson, and my 'nother mother Janette George. And, of course, dear Pinkie.

We get along so well because we're so delightfully different.

The Myth of Normal
(Does anyone believe there is such a thing?)
Preface

In my book about accepting the inevitability of death (and embracing the joy of living), I reached out to everyone who feels fear, frustration, sadness, anxiety, or anger about dying. Here I go again, but this time it's about fears, frustrations, etc. related to "fitting in" with everyone else. It's like I'm on a mission to scrub away all the worries I can find, one book at a time. What am I, some kind of weirdo?

Yes. I have reason to believe people think I'm a misfit, and I agree with them. I see plenty of quirks in others, too, and they see or sense those quirks in themselves. Or, they're oblivious. I'm writing this book for all of us.

Strange as I am, I have loved ones. Why they would love someone like me, I don't know. I love them anyway. Love is a normal thing, which makes it confusing that so many resist saying the word aloud, or deny it or shy away from the feeling, running from it with such force of velocity that their eyes water. As normal as love is, it doesn't fit comfortably into the lives of a surprising number of people.

Every one of us loves and lives and dies, we all eat and sleep and bleed. Sometimes we feel proud of who we are, other times we embarrass ourselves. We're doing the best we can with what we've been programmed by genes to do, or taught by our culture to do, or what we've decided to do despite programming and culture. With all of that in common, we're still inimitably unique.

Our differences define us more fearlessly than

our similarities. There's enough of everyone in me that I want to share back. In other words, the same thing that caused you to pick up this book is the same thing that made me write it. Same thing, only different.

Contents

Introduction 5
Chapter 1: Statistics (Just Kidding) 10
Chapter 2: Seriously. 20
Chapter 3: Judgment Daze 23
Chapter 4: Gendercopiosity 32
Chapter 5: Homophobia, Racism, and Poverty-Bashing 37
Chapter 6: Dreams 44
Chapter 7: Food and other Styles of Fun 51
Chapter 8: Hello Gorgeous 56
Chapter 9: Faith and Politics 65
Chapter 10: You Against the World 73
Chapter 11: Alone and Together 81
Chapter 12: Crime, Guilt, and Punishment 91
Chapter 13: Operator Error 95
Chapter 14: Ethics and Morality 101
Chapter 15: Money and Finances (ways of our world) 105
Chapter 16: Supernatural Superstitions 116
Chapter 17: Connections 121
Chapter 18: The Scintillating Self 128
Chapter 19: Conformity 134
Chapter 20: Compos Mentis? 139
Chapter 21: 149
Warning: This Chapter is NOT Politically Correct 149
Chapter 22: Rascally Children 155
Chapter 23: Whose script is this, anyway? 159
Chapter 24: Creativity (the inexhaustible stuff of living) ...163
Chapter 25: The Psychology of Normal 168
Chapter 26: The Philosophy of Normal 172
Chapter 27: What's the point of all this? 177
MISFIT 195

R.L. George

Introduction

Normal. There's a calmness in that word. It's comforting to hear, "All readings are normal" in just about any context.

"Abnormal" does not invoke a sensation of calm. When used in a phrase it's unnerving, "We have an abnormal reading on the radar, Admiral," or "This is an abnormal x-ray." Context isn't always necessary, either. When one human being looks at another and says a single word, "abnormal," it is rarely if ever a compliment.

By definition, deviating from the norm makes one deviant, which is a concept that often activates contempt, or in more emotional cases, a gag reflex. Even in its simplest form it can be derisive, "Look at all those screaming deviants, topless in the rain!" Sounds like football fans to me, but we all have our own perspective.

Perspective is part of what I'll be talking about here. Where one man sees impropriety another sees sport. One woman's emery board is another woman's sandpaper. The man who's shocked by displays of sportsmanlike passion might be from a land where baring one's chest is an insult, for all we know. And even female construction workers file their nails.

Right there, I separated the sexes, because there's quite a contrast. Many think women and men couldn't be more different if they had come from different planets, but we're all so unique that we may as well each be our *own* planet. We're all in this galaxy but we only travel along with the other planet-humans when they enter our orbit, or when we enter theirs.

Yet we do have a schism of the sexes, and First World countries have taken it to the next extreme by identifying what's called a "gender continuum." One's appearance is often an indicator of gender association but I call **BS** on that. Some women prefer the comfort (and durability) of men's clothes, and some guys are admirably particular about how they dress.

In any event, there's more about appearance than gender identification. For example, I believe all people can be attractive no matter where they fall on any kind of gender continuum, and no matter how they look.

Yes, there is such a thing as attractiveness that has nothing to do with appearance. Handsomeness and beauty, those words can apply to either gender. Surely everyone has seen a beautiful man and a handsome woman.[1] But attractiveness also refers to qualities like charisma, kindness, confidence, kookiness, and other traits that don't start with an alliterative "kuh" sound.

Back to our general differences. For the life of me, I can't see why one attitude is correct and another is wrong, or vice-versa. What you feel inside is the best gauge. The most basic of questions are all one needs to move the needle, such as, "Am I hurting anyone? Hurting myself?" If the answers are "no," then the decisions you make are right, not wrong. You set the limits of your own normal.

Despite those observations we continue to worry about how well we fit in. For example, another cringeworthy word to describe the state of un-normality is "nonconformist." Hippie beads and purple mohawks and sleeve tattoos, I wonder if those or other unusual choices would have been embraced by historical nonconformists? Copernicus, Galileo, Einstein and Tesla. Have people like Steve Jobs and Bill Gates, Robin Williams and Prince ever cringed about their nonconformity?

Those famously unique individuals accepted or ignored their steadfast strangeness in spite of comments about their

---

[1] Although the arguably beautiful Captain Picard was slapped by a woman because he called her "handsome." (Tapestry, 1993.)

clothes, hairdos, or ideas. They kept on being themselves regardless of what kind of support, or disdain, surrounded them. How many in the intimate orbits of those trailblazers accepted them as-is (or as they were), and encouraged their eccentricities? Did anyone try to hold them back, shut them down? In retrospect, the naysayers certainly were put in their place, red-faced if they went public with negative opinions. (The brilliant Nikola Tesla is a convincing example, he had hundreds of patents for his inventions, but his demonstration of a remote-control boat made people cry, "Hoax!" Silly. I don't see why a genius would need to fake anything.)

Fortunately, or regrettably, we don't always say what we think, and we don't act on every thought. Also, our actions often depend on whether our behaviors are private or public.

Is there a difference between how you behave alone versus when you're around other people? Most people admit "Yes," but according to a martial arts sensei I once knew, it's best to behave the same no matter where you are or who you're with. During the course of my lifetime I've learned to agree. Being who you are and trusting that others will accept you is no simple task, but what else have you got? Faking it is too much like lying, countless details can trip one up, and all that falsity is too obvious to real people.

In the end, it isn't worth the effort to lie and pretend.

"Worth," there's a word. What is one's worth? There's no way to have worth as a community if there's no value placed on individuals. Which means it's ironic that communism in Russia, which starts with the letters "commun," is the antithesis of "community." It's also confusing to hear an uproar about "socialism," which is a word that starts with "social." In the meantime, "capitalism" is hailed as the best "ism" in the world. That could be the most logical, because it does miraculously bring billions of people together under a single ideology, but still. When worth is based on income above and beyond sociability, something is fishy in Denmark, South Carolina.[2]

Worth has more than financial implications, of course it does. Conceptions of self and society, including beliefs about good and evil, can help to unwind the finer details of self-worth. Whether or not one is normal is not part of the worthiness equation.

When it comes down to it, intuitive interpretations of normality tend toward one being average, or more fundamentally, not different. Sameness makes me think of porridge for breakfast every morning and boiled meat for dinner every night, with no diversions. If none of us were different we'd all be the same height and weight, wear the same clothes, have the same hairstyles, and our skin colors would be grayish-beige. Oops, I just dozed off.

A more practical definition of "normal" can be found in psychology. It is provocative, and I find psychology's take to be related to mythological or religious expectations, or wishes, or demands made by societies. Many ordinary behaviors in Japan are seen as peculiar in Kenya, and the same can be said of Middle Eastern practices versus Western practices – these universal mismatches represent a fundamental truth about humanity. Normal in one country is outlandish in the next, and that can be narrowed down to ideological mismatches in states or provinces, cities and towns, and within families, too.

Sane. Crazy. Eccentric. Bland. Of those words, the last is the most off-putting to me, and the second-to-last is the most intriguing. Sane is groovy, but eccentric is exciting. Each to his or her own, I suppose.

Aside from psychological definitions, there are also philosophical and scientific attitudes about normality. All three

---

2 There really is a city in South Carolina called Denmark.

of those disciplines have stalwart attitudes about their perspectives, but I'm one who prefers to keep it light and commonsensical.

Time to dig in, but first I'll mention that as I did in the first book in this series, I'll close this one with a fiction piece, the point of which will reflect the rationale of this book: You're different, and that's fine because so is everybody else.

Please remember, it's the most normal thing in the world to wonder about one's own normal-ness. Intentionally trying to be normal is something else altogether. Don Quixote and windmills come to mind. If your intention is sameness, the statistical odds are against success.

Chapter 1: Statistics (Just Kidding)

*The average man exists
only in the statistician's mind.*
– C.C. Smith (in a discussion of Aristotle)

The thing about statistics, other than being hard to pronounce (that might be a personal problem),[3] is that numerical norms are actively sought. That "bell curve" everyone hears about is meant to be a representation of "this is normal," and there are times when numerical tweaking happens for no other reason than to fix that curve. Not-normal is often considered to be a sign of some hidden error.

There will be no numerical tweaking here. I won't be talking much about statistical norms because I have a typical aversion to statistics.

It would make sense to refer to studies and statistical averages in order to tell you how wonderfully outside the norm you are. Or, I could use stats to show you how predictable you are despite your perceived uniqueness. This book is about common sense, though, so my approach will be to talk about real-life observations and comparisons. I prefer exploring likelihoods that arise in humanity through a lens that's intuitive, not mathematical.

I'll arrange this chapter in such a way as to reflect the upcoming pages, starting with some thoughts about the "light and commonsensical" element of my approach. The lightness is in protest of attitudes found in statistics, which is a field that does involve a lot of common sense, but all the analyzing and

---
3 Try saying it three times fast.

overanalyzing makes it oh, so heavy.

    The chapter that will come next is one I thought of titling, "Leave the judgmental attitude at the door," but that sounds snarky, which is not my intention. What I'm referring to in that (now discarded) title is perspective. The best way to gain perspective is to learn about another culture, and the most effective way to do that is to set aside one's own notions about right, wrong, good, bad, indifferent, and normal. It isn't easy to do, but it helps to set aside judgment before stepping inside the spaces where others live in the world.

    If you're in the majority in the place where you're living, that doesn't mean your culture is bigger, or older, than others. Canada, for instance, is a big country with a relatively small population, and it has been a nation for less than 200 years. True, it was a British colony for a bit longer than that, but the climate is much snowier than it is in jolly ole England.

    Despite the shared cultural background of the two countries, the bell curve of how many Canadians take off their shoes when they enter a home has a high middle peak, but there's a much flatter standard deviation in England. To not take off snow-soaked shoes in a Canadian mudroom will cause the housekeeper to shudder, while in England, walking indoors and immediately shedding down to one's socks is likely to draw a polite frown.

    This is why I'll elaborate on why it's best to avoid judging the beliefs of others. Even those who came from the same stock as you can be as different as driving on the left or right side of the road.

    Next will be a chapter on the sexes, which sure can seem 50-50, but the gender continuum has turned any hope of a bell curve into a roller coaster. The percentages are all over the place when it comes to people who are comfortable with society's expectations about how they should behave based on

Myth of Normal

their sex at birth. The statisticians would also be forced to keep tweaking numbers as they move from one culture to the next, and then try to gauge their accuracy despite countries and societies where discussions of gender differences are taboo.

I wish them luck with that. Working from the gut feels like a more effective approach to understanding the evolution of gender. More humanitarian, too.

Statistically, there's bound to be a way to test the potential for an attraction to someone outside one's usual preference. I know some will flinch with discomfort at the idea, and the statistics wouldn't make them feel any better.

No matter what one's gender identification, people get crushes on other people, whether it's a neighbor or coworker or someone famous. With regard to the last, I've heard about a concept of people having "gay crushes" on celebrities, for example a man who has no homosexual impulses whatsoever thinking Anderson Cooper is quite a cutie.[4] What are the odds that someone would be attracted to a person outside their regular preference? No matter what statisticians say, I'd bet a dollar that it happens, at least once in a lifetime, with more than 50% of the population.

Them are fightin' words for some people. "Don't tell me I'm some kind of queer!" Until fairly recently, the word "queer" was only synonymous with words like "peculiar" and "unconventional." Now it has spookier connotations for those who are homophobic, but being homosexual is more unconventional than it is loathsome.

If one wanted to take a statistical look at the details of those who identify as LGBTQ, somewhere between 5% and 10% of human beings fall into that category.[5] Looking at that

---

[4] It could be related to the way Anderson giggles. His giggles—and I mean this in the Irish mythical way—have such a fairy-like quality.

from the low end, 5% of 7 billion inhabitants of Earth is 350,000,000.[6] That's greater than the population of the whole U.S., meaning a whole country's worth of individuals identify as other-than-straight.

Again, some may find all this to be disturbing. Homosexuality is a touchy topic, especially for those who are homophobic. The same is true of the subject of racism (whether one is racist or victimized because of their race), and people from all walks of life are uncomfortable with poverty, too. That can result in what I call, "poverty bashing," but there's also a problem with the impoverished being ignored, or unseen.

With regard to racism, nobody needs statistics to tell them that most of the world is other-than-White. It's easy to compute: China has the largest population, and India is right behind them. The U.S. and countries on the European continent have large populations, but all European citizens combined still can't catch up with China and India. If White racists are smart they'll let their attitude fall by the wayside, because they don't have the numbers to defend against racism that could be aimed toward *them*.

When it comes to poverty, almost half of the world's population lives on a few dollars a day. That's a state of being destitute. Then there's the U.S., where those who live on a few $20s per day are classified as below the poverty level.

Someone might breathe a sigh of relief at being wealthy in a struggling world, but he's still attacked for being the wrong race. Or, he's the dominant race in his society and he's bucks-up, but he's not heterosexual.

Most of us are only ideal human beings in our dreams.

---

5 If all respondents are being entirely honest.
6 Apologies for the accidental number-crunching.

Myth of Normal

Yes, there will be a chapter on dreams. What I just said about being "ideal humans" while dreaming is a milli-fraction of everything else that happens while we slumber. All of dreamland, including "normal," is bizarre. One thing I love about dreaming is statistics are moot. May we never find a way to turn that experience into hard science!

Daydreams are an interesting part of the dream equation. One thing I daydream about all the time is food, which has resulted in a chapter on the subject. Cheese, avocados, a medium-rare filet mignon with a sassy little Claret, I love these indulgences. I would love them if 90% of humanity disagreed with me, and I wouldn't mind that it made me "abnormal."

I'm such a quintessential foodie that it makes me uncomfortable when people aren't excited by eating. Surely something appealing can be found on a given menu, or in the grocery store? Ongoing increases in food varieties have been exponential since the birth of civilization! That's something I wouldn't mind researching someday. I sure did have fun with the chapter on foods and beverages.

However, overindulgence can impact physical appearances. In our society, a fine face doesn't cut it. The bod has to be just right, too. How are we supposed to maintain six-pack abs when there's always a 12-pack of beer in the fridge? Conversely, some say it's worse if the body is beautiful but the face isn't aligned with current trends of gorgeous.

I'm hoping my discussion about what attractiveness is—as viewed internally or externally—will help to elevate self-respect. We all have opinions about our own appearance, and nobody needs numbers to tell them that everyone (who isn't a narcissist) is his or her own worst critic.

And speaking of critics, the chapters following self-image will speak to religion, politics, and what those ideologies look like when they're not one's own.

The idea of conformity is more meaty fodder for this book, and in the chapter on that subject I plan to fully ignore the means and median of those who behave precisely as their world, country, religion, town, or family expects them to behave. Looking at the world versus country versus culture versus self, these make for some fascinating viewpoints.

There are reasons for societal norms, for example attempting to control some of humanity's natural antisocial urges, but those urges to be selfish do remain. The question is not how well one follows expectations, it's whether one is in or out of sync with one's culture. I argue that it's acceptable either way.

After I've exhausted the cultural topic I'll get into how we behave when we're alone as compared to with others. I'm sure there are stats, facts and figures about how much alone time is achieved by those who are married or single, who have children or work for a big company, are in the military or self-employed. The amount of time most people spend alone versus with others is surely calculable, but we can dispense with that and go with our own experiences.

Certain facts won't be central to my point about our behaviors at home, at work, in the grocery store or at a pub, and whether we're being ourselves or trying to do what others expect of us. Commonplace studies about solitude and social behaviors make little difference when it comes to the essence of you. Besides, you have more to worry about than how others are seeing you. How you judge yourself can be more intimidating than any other individual's opinion, more damning than any findings by a jury of your peers.

Self-guilt. Ugh. I would venture to say one's own sense of guilt is more powerful than anything a society can invoke. A good example is the age-old question of morals: Would you do something unethical if you knew you could get away with it? So, you steal or cheat, and you get away with it, now how do you feel? An ethical person would fight demons of guilt for days, years, or decades, depending on the type and size of the crime. Unethical people, as well as sociopaths and the like, couldn't care less. But I doubt they're the type who would read a book like this.[7]

Aside from bearing guilt for consciously committing wrongs, accidental mistakes can also weigh heavily on our minds. However, a Will Rogers quote is appropriate to my opinion about mistakes: "Good judgment comes from experience, and a lot of that comes from bad judgment."

Our ethics and morality are built up in different ways, but they are our own. It would be an impossible task to calculate how many people deviate from their parents' morals, or those of their culture. It's also impossible to know whether deviating would be the best decision. There are too many variables.

As soon as we're old enough to know better, we can own responsibility for all of our errors in judgment. I call that chapter, "Operator Error." I remember how I used to be; when something went wrong my search for the cause went everywhere except the self. I'm old enough to know better, now. Or, there are fair odds that I make more mistakes now, and so they're easier to recognize. Either way, I tend to check myself before I wreck whatever plan or contraption isn't working.

Those contraptions. Appliances, vehicles, computers, they're all at once priceless and pricey. I'll be opining about money and finances in these pages, and how we look at our

---

7   For instance, a narcissist would look at the title and probably think, "Of *course* I'm different! Everyone wishes they could be like me!"

personal situations. The rich want to get richer, the middle class wants to get rich, and the poor want to upgrade from ramen to raviolis. Nobody wants to hear the statistics about how many super-rich there are, because that information reveals how unreachable that goal would be.

Sometimes, there are superstitions behind our goals. This is often obvious in sports, (viz. unwashed jerseys and unclipped beards), but it's sneakier in other areas. Who doesn't wear a lucky shirt or skirt while applying for a job? Why do gamblers ask someone to blow on the dice before they roll? They think it will increase their odds of success. Ha.

Really, a lot of success is more closely related to relations. Family, friends, and other connections we've made are more likely to help us get the best job, meet the right people for dating, even find acceptable homes and cars. Nevertheless, there are those who want to do for themselves, with no outside help. I admire that. It takes courage.

Courage is also required for going against norms. Conformity is king because it allows kings to rule without the messiness. It comes down to how willing one is to go along with the herd. But what I'm trying to establish with this book is the importance of stepping back from the madding crowds to gain a little sanity. When you do that, you may hear words like, "Are you an anomaly?" Don't let it get to you, because everyone is asking the same question of themselves. "Am I the anomaly?"

It's hard to know how to answer that if you've never tried stepping back in order to gain perspective. Some people get caught in the middle, where they're not sure who they want to be. It can be tricky to keep up with which persona belongs where, and sometimes different selves bleed into other territories.

All I can suggest is to stay true to you. I'll repeat an

Myth of Normal

earlier observation: faking it can drive ya crazy.

Crazy, insane, these are spooky words when applied to the self. We need not judge ourselves too hastily, though, because measures of sanity are based on societal norms more often than on some kind of chemical or physiological imbalance. This is another big topic in psychology, but as Sir Isaac Newton said, "I can calculate the motion of heavenly bodies but not the madness of people." Better yet is Mark Twain: "When we remember that we are all mad, the mysteries disappear and life stands explained."

I'm not able to explain bouts of madness but I do hope to alleviate concerns about slips of rationality versus lunacy.

After I explore sane versus not I'll get a little "out there" on my own with a politically incorrect chapter. It comes with a warning, please don't read it if you're worried you'll be offended, or that you'll venomously disagree. Here in this (not) statistics chapter I'll say that a study on what should or should not be okay in a society, or in individuals, and in any given era, would cause a desperate clanging of the bell curves.

That clanging will continue when I move on to the topic of children, but after that will be a few odd chapters that are especially hard on statistics: internal dialogues and creativity.

The last areas I'll be exploring are psychological and philosophical opinions about normality, and that's where statistics really want to try and come into play. "Play" is not the best word, though, because statistics are work. This is why I'm confining about 99% of those number-related concepts to this chapter (and see how few there are here).

Curiously, the odds of being normal are statistically low. Number crunchers can give us an idea of standard height, weight, income, intelligence, and all that, but what's an average attitude? Is there a median for kindness, humility, or sense of humor? There are no reliable measures for how loving a person is, how cunning, sweet-natured, or grumpy. Psychologists try to figure out answers to those questions, but at the moment, there's more clarity in a brick than there is in the scientific vision of human behaviors.

The subject of statistics is no fun. I don't care to know where I would land on the bell curve, and I don't mind knowing I'm probably an outlier in a scatter plot, trailing off the edge of a standard deviation. I'm so different that I'm normal, and I believe that statement can be explained without charts and graphs.

When it comes to people, it's like humor: all a matter of perspective.

Chapter 2: Seriously.

Trouble knocked at the door,
but, hearing laughter, hurried away.
– Benjamin Franklin

We can take ourselves laughably seriously, and it starts for all of us at a very young age. Think back, you're five years old. At school, you sneak away to the bathroom to carefully style a hairdo for picture day, and when you come out, the adults tell you it makes you look like an oddball. Oddball! The nerve. The grownups are laughing but hey, you are deeply offended.

You spent countless minutes on that hairdo, and minutes feel like hours to small children. They don't have years and decades to put time into context, and they also move so much faster than adults do. In the time it takes an adult to gather the grocery bags from the trunk and haul them to the kitchen, a child has changed into shorts, retrieved a toy, grabbed a snack, and is settled in front of the TV.

The adult glances at the TV screen and wishes he could fall into an armchair and stare, but there's the seriousness of putting the milk and meat into the fridge and freezer so they won't go bad, wasting invested dollars. Waste means more hours on the job to pay for overpriced milk and meat.

Serious responsibilities.

Next, a kindergartener who accomplished twenty minutes worth of activity in three minutes and fifteen seconds grows a few years older, to the age of ten. Now, she's teased because she forgot how to spell "of." "Is it u-f? U-v? O-v?" For some reason she can't grab it out of her mind, and she draws that blank at the moment she's writing something on the whiteboard in front of the class.

Now her peers think she's not smart. "Everybody knows how to spell 'of!' What are you, stupid?" She's not stupid, and one day she'll learn that the most common words, names, and birthdays can slip a person's mind.

In the meantime her momentary lapse makes everyone look at her like she's substandard, and it hurts her feelings. The best hope is a dozen years later she can laugh about that lapse, because most English speakers do know how to spell "of," but now she also knows how to spell "hors d'oeuvres" and "peripheral," words that quite a few people get wrong.

Time does its mind-boggling thing of sluggishly blazing by, and we're startled to find that we've reached the age of twenty-one. At that time, we start to accept that the world around us expects us to take ourselves seriously.[8]

Did you join the military, go to college, get a job, fall in love and get married, have a child? There's little frivolity in those endeavors. The military is all about conforming to rules, while in college, too much conformity might be frowned upon.

Well, with regard to that last one, it's not a given. College can be a head-scratcher because "read, listen, regurgitate" still stands as the main method of teaching, but by the time you graduate they require you to have developed an entirely new idea in your discipline. You present your idea and more often than not, all the academicians around you argue about why they don't like it, and you're left with reading, listening, and regurgitating *their* ideas.[9]

Forced scholarly conformity aside, consequential

---

8 Silver spoon kids notwithstanding.
9 I wonder if there's an algorithm that can catch my complaints about academia and pop-up a "no whining!" command whenever I go there.

decisions that must be weighted with gravity include finding the right job or spouse, having a child or two, following a plethora of religious and societal laws, and so forth. When do we get to relax and laugh a little?

We can retrospectively laugh when we see ourselves at age five wearing a horizontally-spiked hairdo, or remember misspelling "of" at age ten. Memories of cheer and achievement arise after graduating boot camp or college, and we smile radiantly when we fall in love, get married, and have children. It can be seriously pleasurable to follow the conventions of adulthood, but then it becomes disconcerting when people question how solemn you are.

"Really?" is what some will ask when you want to camp in the back yard instead of taking the RV somewhere. "Are you kidding me?" is a response that can arise when you suggest going to Disney World instead of hunting for dates on a singles' cruise.

It can be hard on us when our tastes are compared with what others perceive good taste to be.

Is it acceptable to enjoy cartoons as an adult, rather than dramas, documentaries or news shows? Should we stop wasting time with MPRPGs?[10] Are we crazy because we'd rather not get a college degree, or loco if we have no interest in marrying, raising children, buying a house?

I'm a great fan of you doing you, as you are, no matter what everyone else thinks you should be doing. When the judgment of others weighs on you, I hope you can draw on humor to lighten those loads. Never suppress the urge to say or do things that send you into fits of giggles. Actively seek out the instances when you're inspired to send a text that says,

---

10 Multi-Player Role Playing Games. I wish I had the time for that, it is some exciting virtual reality!

"roflmao."

And please, when you see other playful adults, please try not to judge them.

Chapter 3: Judgment Daze

*Thinking is difficult,
that's why most people judge.*
- Jung

The title of this chapter refers to the dizzying topic of sending or receiving judgmental thoughts, and subsequent responses. In real life, it's difficult to follow the biblical edict, "Judge not, that ye be not judged."[11] Thoughts can bounce and tumble when we first meet someone, and/or after we get to know them over time.

Assumptions erupt around those who are different, for example seeing a heavily bejeweled person dressed in a dramatic fashion, speaking in strange voices, excessively smiling all the while.[12] I honestly don't know how we can program our thoughts to a point of being able to avoid judging the people around us.

By itself, the word "judge" isn't ugly, as beauty contest judges will attest. In fact, the contestants in beauty contests are specifically requesting judgment, and the same is true of other playful, positive, or beneficial situations. College students pay— and build up quite a fistful of debt—to have their work judged by professors.[13]

Anyone who says, "Do these clothes make me look fat?" is asking for judgment (and anyone who answers "yes" is just asking for it). Kids who bring their artwork home feel that

---

11 Matthew 7:1.
12 I just described Lily Tomlin.
13 No academic whining!

it has been judged as Louvre-worthy when it gets magnetized to the fridge. (Maybe it's only French kids who think that way, while artsy American kids think of the MMA.)[14]

No matter how judgment is defined, the way others see us, and the way we see others, is both universal and subjective. The universality is to do with all of us being seen from the outside in, and it's subjective because we can only ever see from the inside out. These perspectives mix and tumble in many ways.

He sees her as a sexy goddess and she sees him as an oaf, he sees himself as a beefcake and she sees herself as bookish. Teens who feel all grown up see adults as old fogies, but those teens are simultaneously aggravated because most adults see teens as children. Students are brimming with ideas when they enter school, while teachers see them as empty vessels to fill.

The best teachers continue learning, eventually tapping into the adage about how humbling it is to become aware of how little one knows. The best students of all ages figure out that if their mental cup is filled to the brim, new information won't fit. Incoming knowledge spills over, wasted, leaving a slippery mess that must be cleaned up before it causes an indelible stain of ignorance and narrow-mindedness.

Knowledge and wisdom can put the kibosh on the urge to judge because one gains a refrain of, "I need more information before I can make a reasonable conclusion."

Misconceptions that come from a lack of knowledge happen all the time, and from all different angles.

I remember when I was a kid hearing about Hell's Angels, I'd see biker guys in long beards and leathers, much of their visible skin covered with tattoos. They intimidated the

---

14 As in Metropolitan Museum of Art, not Mixed Martial Arts.

Myth of Normal

tween and teenaged me. Fast-forward a few decades and guys in long beards and leathers may be members of the **LGBTQ** community, and a big business **CEO** has tattoos peeking out from the cuffs of her power suit.

Everything is always in transition, we're swept up in a constant flow of the world changing and its people adapting. Appearances can deceive. There you are thinking you're all caught up with the latest trends in society, and then you're "woke" to something wholly new to you, something that is abruptly and fleetingly hip, bodacious, rad, cool, slick, sick, or on fleek. (Who'd've thunk it would be a happenin' thang for kids to be flossing?)[15]

You can be a half-step behind the latest thing at every stage of life.

We become conscious of trying to keep up in school, our first big social environment. Everyone looks at each other and wonders who they are based on the status of grades or physical acumen, or how clothes and hair are worn and styled. Most distressing of all is wondering what everyone else is saying about each other.

I wish I could imprint it on the mind of every teenager that adulthood may be a year or two away, but it is light years from high school. If I were a **MPRPG** game programmer I would build in a subliminal message to every player under the age of 18: "Adulthood is not. at all. like school."

Looking out from the inside of a popular group, or looking in from outside, we judge the "others." She's slow-witted, or he's empty-headed, someone is too smart or shy or aggressive, the list is long and it boomerangs from the outside to the insider-group and back again, it's a nauseating spin.

It is all spin. Our judgment is saturated with perspective.

---

[15] Dance not dental.

R.L. George

Vistas are narrowed by point of view. There's that East Indian story of the blind men and the elephant, where each of them compares his perception with elements that really have nothing to do with elephant-ness. The trunk inspires the image of a snake, the ear is a magic carpet, the tail a piece of rope.

Each of the elephant men only experience part of the animal, as we humans only experience parts of the world. Those who travel often bring their suppositions with them, too. I've seen or heard of visitors in other countries assuming it doesn't matter how one greets another, or which hand is best used for eating, or how to properly thank someone for a kindness.

Many Europeans greet with air kisses or real kisses on the cheeks, but if a Swiss woman kisses a single Mexican man three times when she greets him, he may suspect it's a romantic gesture. A married Mexican man would find his eyes darting around for the location of his own wife, while a French husband would return the cheek kisses of the Swiss man who just kissed his wife.

What I mean to say is the Frenchman kissed the wife of the Swiss man and then the Swiss man kissed the Frenchman in greeting... It isn't a sexual advance in Europe, but if a Frenchman kisses the wife of his Japanese boss, would the boss still feel inclined to bow?

I think he would. It depends on how well the Japanese boss has learned about the norms in other nations, but surely he wouldn't be an international boss if he didn't have a mind that expands beyond his own society's norms.

In Indian and Muslim countries it's customary to use only the right hand for eating, because the left hand is used in the bathroom. If someone in India stops you from using your left hand to grab your masala sandwich, thank her—unless she's your sister. In India it's insulting to thank someone who's close

Myth of Normal

to you, because their loving help is a given. (It must be confusing to say to a parent, "Yes, I could use your loving help, but I'm not going to thank you for it.")

It's hard to know all the minutiae of what's okay and what's not in different parts of the world. This is the reason it's best not to judge someone who moves in for a kiss of greeting, pushes a sandwich into your right hand, and then wordlessly takes a $100 rupee loan from his Ma. How is anyone expected to keep up with the details?

Books, television, movies, and streamed entertainment provide a minimum of worldwide reality. This is why fiction is described with words like "fabricated" and "not true." Really, how many Crazy Rich Asians are there? How often do impoverished contestants win a million on a game show in India? How realistic is the type of family portrayed in This Is Us?

Somebody could speak up and say, "There's such a thing as Asians who are rich and crazy, and surely at least one East Indian has won a million on a game show. There must be one or two families that are very much like the people in This Is Us."

Sure. Exceptions undergird my point. We are all exceptions to every rule. There are wealthy lunatics but they're from a hundred different countries, and the countries that broadcast game shows undoubtedly reward their contestants well, at least once or twice. It happens.

Each family is so unique that we could make a show about yours, mine, his, hers, and theirs. You'd be gasping and chuckling and sobbing each week at the comic tragedy of us all, would that we could portray every family on Earth! Empathy would become the divine driving force of humanity.

I've had friends who learned about my family and said, "Wow, they're a bit much, aren't they?" All I need to say is,

"Tell me about your family." The response is always to the effect of, "Oh, I get it. Never mind."

Here's a quote from Rita Mae Brown: "The statistics on sanity are that one out of every four people is suffering from a mental illness. Look at your three best friends. If they're okay, then it's you." Insightful (and funny) as that observation is, it can also start loopy arguments of, " *You're* the crazy one." "No, *you* are."

It occurs to me that I've had that very exchange with friends, but we weren't arguing. When we said "crazy" it was more complimentary, as if we were saying, "You're the coolest one." "No, *you* are."

When it comes down to it, the way we are with friends and family cannot be duplicated, but there are similarities.

Think back to when you were very young, under ten years old. Did it seem that all the families around you were gloriously loving and flawlessly balanced? Only yours was a little off-kilter, wobbly and stumbling through the days and years with oh so much stress and woe, too many troubles. Yes?

If that's how you remember it, don't get spooked thinking I've researched your family through 23andMe. Odds are, many young children from the homes around you were lumping your house or apartment in with the "rest of the neighborhood," thinking your life couldn't possibly be as complicated as their own.

That position often expands into wholly different cultures, although it's an opposite effect. Rather than feeling like an outsider we see other cultures as bizarro, and we're relieved to be inside the normal group. It comes back to perspective, though. We see people in other lands through the lens of our society, and although their norms look outlandish to us, I imagine they see us in the same way.

What's normal for you is abnormal for them, and vice-versa. American children hide their teeth under their pillows, you smile when you give someone a thumbs up, and We the People laugh out loud so often that "lol" is one of the first and best known electronic abbreviations. Somewhere else baby teeth are thrown off the roof, and up-tilted thumbs are more like a middle finger delivered with a scowl when someone grabs your parking spot. And the funny thing about laughter is about five years ago, a Turkish Deputy Prime Minister told women not to laugh in public.[16] I can almost hear the women's reaction, haha.

Nuttier still is the official—whose ridiculousness went further than anti-laughterism—*won* his high office. He wasn't appointed, therefore he must have been considered normal by a large faction of people who voted for him. It's my hope that those who initially agreed with his ideas changed their minds after his laughter ban, especially while sharing jokes with sisters in parks, reminiscing with mothers in restaurants, or hearing the sound of joy at daughters' weddings.

Learning by experience is an ongoing process, and it's as pleasurable as it is painful. It hurts to realize, and then admit, that one is wrong. Hearing that your chosen leader wants to ban something as healthful and joyful as laughing is disconcerting. However, it eases the pain of acknowledging your error when you experience the pleasure of hearing your infant daughter blissfully giggling.

Yes, it's embarrassing, in retrospect, to have supported the "no women laughing in public" fella, but it would be agony to see your female loved one holding a constantly dour expression.

Judging someone to be our best representative is a

---

16 I read about this in a 2014 Huff Post story by Harut Sassounian. Cracked me up.

difficult task, and subsequently learning that person is loathsome can be humiliating. It comes up when we choose to date or marry, too, where we sometimes find out she or he is a fink on some level or another.

Somehow, mature and experienced adults are capable of misjudging even their own children, and here's the kicker: we can also misinterpret our very selves.

That's a challenge that comes up in therapy. Someone walks in with certain self-assumptions, like, "I'm a terrific co-worker and I'm great with my kids, I'm just having a little trouble with stress." The therapist does a whole workup and announces, "You're bi-polar," or "clinically depressed" or, gasp, "schizophrenic."

Nobody wants to hear anything like that. You live an entire life thinking you know yourself, and who could know you better? Apparently professionals can, physical doctors being a popular example. They (ideally) offer a proper diagnosis of that ache or twinge, and they can set that broken arm. They might know how to calm a stomachache or soothe stuttering breaths. But head doctors? The jury is still in deliberation about the correctness and effectiveness of their diagnoses and cures.

It's a shock to hear you're something you've never suspected yourself to be. You've misjudged yourself. There's always a chance the doctor is wrong, but they don't come up with their diagnoses lightly. When therapy works (whether it's talking or pharmaceutical), that's a sign of it being a correct diagnosis.

A practical application of what I'm saying swings me back to the point of this chapter about judgmentality. When you judge someone's personality, it's not unlike a psychological diagnosis. However, "He's a sociopath" or "She's a humorless shrew" is hard to prove until time and talk become part of the

Myth of Normal

equation.

The more I think about it, the clearer it is: as quickly as I judge people, they're judging me back. I don't like the feeling and so I can assume they don't like it either. None of us know when we'll learn that something about us is off a tick, so why pick on others? We're all one life-changing tragedy away from PTSD, we could be harboring a gene for clinical depression, and even if we survive the whole rollercoaster of life we may find dementia at the end of the ride.

That's a bleak argument for avoiding judgmental behaviors. I'd rather say, have pity on those you're tempted to judge because they're one act of kindness away from gaining your respect.

It's hard to tell who anybody will turn out to be, whether it's strangers, friends, family members, or the person you see in the mirror. Brace yourself: the same is true of gender.

R.L. George

Chapter 4: Gendercopiosity[17]

*Gender is between your ears
and not between your legs*
– Chastity Bono

The reason I agree with the quote for this chapter is that we once used "sex" to anatomically differentiate between male and female. Now we used the word "gender" to cover that basic definition of, "he has male and she has female anatomy." In reality, gender used to refer exclusively to differences in one's societal or cultural (rather than anatomical) traits and behaviors. Now we're associating it with one's very own traits and behaviors, honoring the way each individual interprets the reflection in the mirror.

American society identifies the color blue with males and pink with females, making you abnormal if you're an American who prefers the color opposite your sex. That would not be true, though, if you were in the same society 200 years earlier, when pink was associated with males. The only reason Americans assign the colors as we do is because advertisers made it popular, and that was after a few trial runs.

What this means is you're not universally abnormal if you're a male who likes pink, because that was once commonplace. A pink-lovin' guy would have normal 200 years ago, he'd have been outside the norm 50 years ago, but he might be like most other guys 50 years from now (which may

---

17 I like to make up words. It was pretty challenging to come up with one about gender that hasn't been used yet! This one combines the "copia" of abundance with an "opia" of seeing, and the "osity" of simply being.

be helped by the fact that many big, strong, masculine football players wear pink during Breast Cancer Awareness month).

My suggestion is to like what you like without concerning yourself about what's popular. If what you like is out of phase now, it was once fine and it will be fine again, someday. Women can love physics (Madame Curie) and mathematics (Katherine Johnson). Men can get into sobby love stories (they do star in them, after all), and plenty of guys are fine with raising children (Cary Grant and David Beckham are examples from two different generations).

Most can intuit that women would have loved to be in the workplace sooner than they were allowed, and since time immemorial, there have been men who wished they could stay home while their wives won the bread. It makes me sigh to think of how many people have been skewered to their assigned responsibilities, feeling that they had to follow the norms or face persecution.

Nowadays the world benefits from nurturing males and powerful women. Look into the eyes of an adult who was raised by a kind, loving father and see the self-worth, the integrity. Same goes for the strength and compassion that can be seen in children of hardworking single mothers. Switching things up, down, and sideways often has positive results. Locking people into roles often has negative results.

If you're comfortable in the roles assigned to you, good on ya! On the other hand, I worry about those who are fine with conforming to every single thing others instruct or expect them to do, to think, to be. A healthy sense of self is what informs your particular life, and self is bound to come into conflict with the external expectations that surround you like a mold.[18]

---

18 I meant that as a predetermined form, but I guess it could also be like a

R.L. George

I bring up the people who are okay with their assigned gender because I wouldn't want someone to read this and be shut down the moment they disagree. Yet even if you are content with being the poster-girl/boy for your anatomical sex, there's bound to be something else in your life that feels like a disconnect. Not tall or slender or strong enough, too aggressive (for a woman) or shy (for a guy). It's exceptional for anyone to think she or he is perfect, but I bet you're not thinking that because I doubt perfect people would read a book like this.

More on perfection later, for now I'll stick with how we think about gender identification.

This is a gut-hit, but there's probably an "average" when it comes to women who would love to have a career as much as children, and average men are the same. Family, work, security, that's what most of us want. Both sexes belong in the kitchen because hey, people need to eat food. It's a good idea for both sexes to work because living is expensive, don't we all know it.

There's no reason a woman shouldn't be a mechanic. Slender fingers can fit into the narrow spaces that are a facet of mechanical inventions. Men are great at cleaning the bathroom because they have a better idea of where some speckles accidentally landed in the middle of the night.

The average woman does not wear a size zero and smoky-eye makeup, she does not have sublimely styled hair every single day, and her fingernails have flaws. The average man does not have a washboard stomach, a six-figure income, and his fingernails can look nice (not necessarily feminine) when they're filed and polished.

Fingernails, long hair, baldness, finances, physicality and

---

fungus. Both can make it hard to breathe.

appearance. These are some of the ways we distinguish masculine from feminine individuals, but that is not a constant. Well, except for finances, I guess. Apparently there's still a gap in wages, but that's bound to get fixed someday. Of course. Sure it will. If not, there's always the Lysistrata option.[19]

A number of notably masculine guys have made manscaping and man-buns a hunky thing. Confident women who shave their heads to near-baldness can be extraordinarily sexy, and piercings and tattoos are becoming universal in some First World societies. Nothing is sacredly male or female anymore (except giving birth, and who knows what technology will bring)?

Being yourself with no shame or regrets is not as simple as it sounds. However, it feels better—and it looks better—than trying to stumble around inside proscribed lines. Since time immemorial, people who are gay or transgender have been forced to fake it and do what their society requires. Actually, it often didn't require force, because people tend to try and do whatever is necessary to fit in. Even today, as societies evolve, LGBTQ people have giant walls to climb before they find the nerve to tell family members, coworkers, and anyone else in their sphere.

By comparison, it's a walk in the park for a woman to decide she'll wear cozy shoes instead of heels, or for a man to cry at a movie because it genuinely moved him to tears.

We get what we're given when we're born, and I'm referring to more than the identifying organs that indicate male or female. The start of life includes all sorts of adult behaviors that show you how to be male or female, and it's assumed that

---

[19] Aristophanes' ancient Greek comedy: a group of women withhold sex from their husbands to force them to end their warring ways, but I see no reason why that tactic wouldn't work for any other crucial negotiation.

you'll respond appropriately to those expectations. Veiled instructions and outright modeling behaviors are based on what one's given society is commanding. Society doesn't always command what's best for individuals, though, because the point is to get everyone to coalesce, to fuse together into a community.

Luckily, communities aren't stagnant. As each human being grows, so do the societies surrounding them. We'd struggle if we were dropped into to 1300s England just as they'd be a little freaked out by the U.S. in the 21st century. We'd be like, "No lights, no plumbing, no cars, no phones, say what?" and they'd be saying, "Lights and plumbing are such wonders of the future, but everybody goes from houses into rolling boxes to work, and then back into the rolling boxes... when do they get exercise? And why does everybody stare at their technological machines rather than into each other's eyes?"

Evolution means more than technology, of course. Our visitor from the olden days also learns that the person with a buzz-cut isn't necessarily a boy, and the one wearing a bun doesn't have to be a girl. Unlike people from the 1300s we've come to understand that the way a person looks is an *expression*, not a *definition*, of their personality.[20]

Time and place put everything into perspective. The more we learn, the more we know how to accept everyone we haven't met yet. I'm not immune to the fact that it can be scary to accept someone who's wholly different from you, but please start with curiosity rather than prejudice.

---

20 I know, that's another way of saying you can't judge a book by its cover, but they didn't have much in the way of books in 1300s England.

Chapter 5: Homophobia, Racism, and Poverty-Bashing

> *Do we have to worry about who's gay
> and who's straight?
> Can't we just love everybody
> and judge them by the car they drive?*
> – Ellen DeGeneres

    This won't be the easiest chapter in this book, whether it's on my end (writing it) or on your end (reading it). The title gives an idea of some types of anti-otherisms that occur, but people can also be marginalized because of their religion, body size, political attitude, income level, etc., etc., and sadly, etc. again.

    I'll start with income. The U.S. is a capitalist society that tries to find ways of helping the less fortunate, and yet we often judge the poor as inadequate. I suppose it's true that some people are just lazy, but in my experience, they're the minority among the poor. As is true with every socioeconomic faction, some may wish for work that doesn't take much effort, but most like having something meaningful to do.

    Given a choice, would you prefer to sit around broke and bored, or do some work in order to afford a reliable car, a nice TV, gourmet popcorn, and on a good day, Elite Vienna bonbons?

    I don't think laziness is as common as some say it is, and when it's associated with an entire ethnicity, I'm stunned by the audacity. Only brainwashing, rumors, and propaganda can make anyone believe a whole race can have a single defining characteristic. Purposely creating hateful attitudes and behaviors borders on evil. Ironically, I believe even bigoted people can agree with that.

Hundreds of years ago, Europeans and Americans went to Africa as slavers. Should every African have thought of all light-skinned people as monstrous? Absurd. Equally absurd is the idea that a hardworking person of color is rare. The fact that people really do think that way, it astonishes me. Especially when someone who thinks that way has never interacted with a person of color.

While living in Canada I witnessed bigotry toward Native Americans. If that surprises you, welcome to my world. I didn't know what to make of it. I also experienced prejudice toward *me*, because I'm from the States, and many Canadians didn't care for the president who happened to be in office at the time. I tried to explain that leaders couldn't possibly be the prototype of every citizen of their country, but they brushed me off. Then they returned to grousing about the Native Americans in Canada.[21]

I've also heard wretched references to Mexicans being lazy. When I lived in Mexico I found that the southern heat forced businesses to close their doors during the most sizzling part of the day, which happens to be the peak of the workday for many U.S. citizens. That doesn't mean doors were closed for the rest of the night.

Businesses opened in the early morning when it was still cool. They stayed open until 2 or 3pm, and if you started at 6am and closed at 2, that means 8 hours right there. When the blistering heat descended it was siesta time, which reminds me of another misconception: sleeping in the middle of the day sounds like an indolent way to live. However, the locals usually rose and reopened their doors in the evening, adding

---

21 Yes, my logic also applies to the Canadians I'm describing, who most certainly don't represent *all* Canadians.

more time to those 8 hour days.

Incidentally, one of the best things about the area where I lived in Mexico is that everyone judged one another based on personality, not income. I'm not sure if that holds true today, or in other regions, but in my experience, it was an eye-opening way to live.

Assumptions that are made about different ethnicities are unrealistic. It would be the same as saying all blue-eyed people are immature, or black dogs are smarter than white dogs. Preposterous.

When it comes to domestic pets, some might argue that animals can be bred to be smarter. Is that true of humans? If so, it would involve mixing races. Inbreeding in humans has been historically shown as dangerous. The offspring of siblings and cousins have been found to suffer from genetic disorders, and although scientists use mouthfuls of words like "homozygous" and "consanguinity," the human race has witnessed tangible results.

Royal families have been afflicted with hemophilia, mental illness, infertility, and more. They engaged in inbreeding because they wanted to keep their bloodlines "pure," yet it turned out to be a toxic practice. The human race knows that's true because there it is, physical evidence in royal bloodlines.

It's confusing that to this day, individuals are deeply concerned with maintaining their racial purity. Why would people ignore the evidence that it's detrimental, and may even cause them to die out?

My theory is that there's a primal human memory of royalty claiming to have descended from gods, and so "pure" blood meant an intimate relationship with the divine. That the inbreeding resulted in so many genetic problems raises the question of whether royals really are related to the gods, which are supposed to be flawless superhumans. Nevertheless, the history of racial purity and superiority has remained embedded in the human psyche.

Human history of the gods, or one God, is rife with conflict. National and international wars have been waged in the name of religion. Weirdly, even people who are racist have been known to set aside the kinship of matching skin-color if someone is worshiping the wrong god.

There's the Catholic/Protestant schism in Ireland, and there's the timeless persecution of Jews, including the era of the Inquisition, an institution that also tormented Muslims. Mormons, Christian Scientists, Scientologists, snake handlers, and atheists have borne the brunt of discrimination. The list goes on and on, so much so that it can be called normal for us to attack each other in the name of religion.

There's no little irony that it's normal to be religious, and the word "normal" is associated with "sane," but we have gotten into some cuh-razy wars over spiritual beliefs.[22]

Those who are advocates of racial purity and religious uniformity claim to see behavioral differences in skin color, and they're convinced they can identify religious affiliation by facial features and hair type. Some believe they can also tell whether a person is homosexual by relying on "gaydar."

None of these judgments are reliable. For example, what does a lesbian look like? When I lived in Canada I saw countless stocky, muscular women with very short hair, and yet most of them had a husband and a child or two. I remember wondering why anyone would prefer short hair when long hair could add to warmth. No ready answer came from anyone I talked to about it, so I decided it must be associated with a freaky image of long hair blown out by sub-zero winds.

---

22 As C.G. Jung once said, "Show me a sane man, and I will cure him for you."

Myth of Normal

Heavy coats and layers of clothing also added to the stocky appearance of Canadian women. I'm guessing that trudging or skiing through snow helps build muscle, too. Plus there's lots of firewood to cut in Canada.

In my personal experience, the duties of surviving intense Canadian winters were not based on one's sex. Everybody had to do whatever work required to stay warm, which included men tucking babies inside their coats and women pushing a car out of a snowbank.

Despite realities like this around the world, someone who believes in racial, sexual, and religious purity can take the next step and look at women as inferior. Now we have a guy who only likes people who match his skin color and attends the same men-led church that's filled with heterosexual worshipers. Seems that such a world would be awfully small.

Another step is for the guy to look at the same-color heterosexual man who believes in the same god – but no, *that* fellow won't do, because his politics are so wrong he should be imprisoned. He's obese, t'boot, and we can't have that. And he smokes cigarettes, *gah*, surely he's trying to kill us all with those firesticks!

That guy would have so few people left. "Narrow demographics" is actually a deal-breaker advertising concept, with fewer options equaling fewer sales. Same goes for narrowing the field of personal relationships. The more we nitpick the individuals around us, the fewer friends we'll have.

The number of flawed people walking around this world is staggering, but what astonishes me more is the way flaws can be seen as bulls-eyes. When your difference is visible, like your height or the color of your skin, it cannot be hidden or faked. It's not possible to change one's essential self. When people wish you harm because of that impossible-to-change appearance, it's hellish.

Those who are flagrantly homosexual have similar difficulties. It wouldn't be easy for a feminine woman to "become" masculine, and the same is true of feminine men. It would be like a naturally surly person feigning perkiness, and vice-versa. Some try to behave in a way that's different from their characteristics but c'mon, they aren't fooling anyone. Not even themselves.

The author Rita Mae Brown was onto something when she said, "The only queer people are those who don't love anybody." Do bullies love anyone? Surely they do, and I wish they'd ask themselves how they'd feel if their loved one was bullied.

All of the visual impacts I describe above can bring on abuse, and the same is true of suppositions. To be accused of laziness for the sole reason that your skin isn't white is ludicrous. It sets a precedent for future anti-others ideas. Indicators of individual value will be the foods they eat, the size of their teeth, whether they drink coffee or tea.[23]

Sound silly? No sillier than the current prejudices against, say, extremely short people. That could morph into bigotry against all males who are under six feet tall. Women who are over six feet tall could be next on the list. Unbelievable? Straight hair versus curly hair has already been a thing, as is the size of one's nose or lips, or the shape of one's eyes.

No difference is too small for humans who tend toward bigotry. The sad truth is if they keep it up, there will come a day when one of their own traits will be found substandard.

When I was in my teens and early twenties, a budding humanitarian, I used to say, "I'm not bigoted against anybody

---

[23] I did once hear that men who drink tea instead of coffee are seen as "not manly enough" in some professions.

Myth of Normal

except bigots." By the time I reached my my thirties I tossed that idea out of my head. I don't want to be bigoted against *anyone*.[24] How could bigots learn to be otherwise if they never see what acceptance looks like? Their anger must be intensified when others scowl at them. I erased my bigotry against bigots; I'd rather model acceptance.

We have no choice but to be different. Musician Hayley Williams said, "If we were meant to be the same then we wouldn't be human." It makes more than a little sense, because if we were all alike, that would mean there would be only one sex. Presumably that sex would be able to reproduce, but you'd have to procreate with people who look exactly the way you do. And what would happen when school let out? Your children would need to locate you by your clothes or car rather than your face.

Irrational. Fantastical. Nightmarish.

Surely we can do better than live such nightmares while we're awake!

---

24 Although I will listen to arguments about being bigoted against bullies... Wait. Maybe bigotry against bully*ing* is the way to go.

R.L. George

Chapter 6: Dreams

Man is a genius when he is dreaming.
- Akira Kurosawa

Dreams are a manifestation of magic. We're in a state of unconsciousness, and yet we're not. While asleep we're (mostly) unaware of the world around us, yet we possess awareness in our dreams. Our ancient ancestors associated dreams with a higher power, and my science hero Sir Roger Penrose has theories about dreaming and consciousness that are based on quantum physics.

There's an old skit about a wife slugging her husband because he dreams about his favorite movie star. It's as though he's having an affair. Is he? The star must be on his mind, yes? He admires her beauty and appreciates her talents, but would he have an affair with her if he met her in the flesh? Probably. Wait, I mean he probably would not, if all we're going on is his dream about her. Whether or not he's a scoundrel while awake is another question.

When I first said the guy would probably act on his attraction in person, my Freudian slip was showing. Freud was literally involved when I popped out with "probably," because he's the one who said dreams are wish fulfillment. If the husband finds someone attractive it's likely he would wish to pursue it, but most of us try to show some measure of restraint in our waking lives.

All that said, I disagree with Dr. Freud. Dreams are so much more than acting out wishes.

I've dreamed entire storylines set in different eras, in color, black-and-white, and sepia. I sometimes fly in my dreams, and I'm not necessarily stuck within Earth's atmosphere while flying. I suppose that could be a type of wish fulfillment, but some of the storylines I've dreamed? Not at all.

A sepia-colored dream I once had was set in the late 1800s southwest, and it had a beginning, a middle, and an end. It was a coherent story. I was not a part of the story in the dream, I was an observer, but it wasn't a subject of any great interest to me. I've never had a wish to be anything like any of the characters, and the era and location hold no special interest for me.

Wishes were in no way a part of that dream experience. It was like a movie you find on a rainy day when you have nothing pressing to do, and you accidentally left the remote in the kitchen, and you're too tuckered out to change the channel by hand.

I was about to move right on to thoughts about the sources of certain dreams, but it occurs to me that if I were a stranger reading the above paragraphs I'd be thinking, "So what was the sepia dream about, already?"

Although this really was movie length, with all sorts of details, I'll summarize it here: A man owned a bank with a partner. The man was married to a woman who stayed at home all day, and he was mean to her in a way that had to do with neglect and excessive condescension. One day the man found that his partner had left a huge satchel of money on the bank's counter, and decided he would teach him a lesson. He hauled the package home with him at lunchtime and hid it in the house without telling his wife anything about it. However, on his way back to the bank, a horse and carriage runs him over and kills him.

Again, this was the late 1800s in the southwest. People were sometimes killed by horse-drawn carriages.

It gets to the point where the partner goes to the wife to offer his condolences, but he also has to tell her that the bank owns everything in her world. The house, furniture, dishes, even her clothes. She'll have to move on, and there's no way he can help her because he's in a fix: someone stole a big, heavy satchel of money from the bank.

The partner leaves and the wife is bereft. It isn't that she misses her dullard of a husband so much, but how will she survive? As she's wandering through the house in despair she stumbles upon the money. She is an honorable woman, and she's friendly with the partner (despite his well-mannered but rude dismissal of her). Will she return the money to him?

At the end of my southwest movie-dream there's a train (*quelle surprise*), and the woman is standing at the station. She's wearing the dress she owned when she met her husband, and she's carrying a single suitcase. It's a big, heavy suitcase. The End.

No idea why I had that dream. There was also no wish fulfillment, no prophecy, not a rehash of my day. It had nothing to do with anything I have ever experienced.

Now that I think about it, that might not have been the best example of my dreams, many of which are truly amazing. I'll add another quick one that had nothing to do with anything I've ever seen or experienced, and it was simply this: I went into a beautiful, green valley where there were many people waiting in an extremely long line to offer gifts to a blond boy, I think he was in his early teens. I found a big palm leaf and filled it with some fruits I found, and joined the line. When I reached the boy he shyly accepted the gift from me. He understood that everyone wanted to honor him, but he was humble.

That was it. What a dream, yes?

I do think it would be fun if I could relax and dream

homemade movies on demand. Or fly, for that matter. Before I fall asleep tonight, I'm going to seed my mind with those ideas. Whether or not it will work is unknown.

Scientifically, dreams are bound to be seeded by everything that floods into our consciousness each day. Freud's idea of wish fulfillment has the ring of truth, too. It's less likely that we dream prophecies, but those who believe they've had the experience would debate that statement. Another theory is that there are quantum events occurring that cause us to phase in and out of different dimensions, or time-streams, while we're dreaming.

Which is it?

I'm convinced that the mix of science, psychology, theology, magic, and the mythological mysteries of the human brain are all influencing our dreams. Now that I think about it, that one sentence is a good summation of the East Indian mathematician Ramanujan. He claimed some of his scientific formulas came to him in dreams from the goddess Namagiri.

It's all right there in that one example: mathematics; psychological influences; a goddess; and the myth and magic of Namagiri contacting Ramanujan. All of those mysterious events are culminated in the physiology of a dreaming human brain. Although interestingly, the climax of my example is not the dream but the practical applications that came from Ramanujan dreaming. He did stimulate a whole lot of mathematicians, who went on to provide fodder for today's technology.

I'm sure there's a biological answer to how and why we dream, it's only a matter of time before we identify the facts. There's bound to be some rigorous approach that can provide a number-crunchable answer to the science of dreaming but oh, ouch, that's so arid I just had a dry sneeze.

I can see why we'd want to know why we sneeze, but I'm

not sure why we must know things like, say, how the act of walking propels us in any direction we choose. The why of what we do isn't as important as the beneficial effects, such as expelling a dusty mote of science from one's nose or moving from the armchair to the refrigerator.

The importance of knowing why we dream, on a scale of 10, is about a 6. The fact that we do have dreams is a 10. My opinion on this is clear, yet there is a question as to why I give knowledge about dreaming as much as a 6 on a scale of 10.

For one thing, Roger Penrose's theories about accessing different dimensions while dreaming is titillating. Finding a way to do some inter-dimensional investigations would be worth erasing some of the enhantment of dreaming, because it would open a whole new realm of magic.

Secondly, learning about biological dream processes could come in handy because nightmares are hard to take. I'm not convinced we should try to make them go away, because everything (even a nightmare) happens for a reason. Yet knowing how to control the adverse effects of bad dreams would help a lot of people who are suffering, night after night.

Whatever is going on in your nightmares or dreams, what does it say about you? What is it that your dreams can tell you? Is there any such thing as normal dreaming? Apparently there is.

According to scholars who talk about this sort of thing, it's normal to fall asleep and find yourself in an alternative reality. During the dream, normal dreamers don't know they're in a reality that is not of this world. They interact with fully formed characters who they've never met in waking life, and time bounces around like a pinball that burst through the glass of its machine. Animals can talk, newborn babies can walk, family members come back from the dead, and in the dream, the dreamer is usually fine with all of these miraculous developments.

Sounds kind of schizophrenic, but there it is.

The dreams you have can provide insights into what you wish could happen, or what you're trying to keep secret from yourself (or from your wife). Your dreams could be an indication of how creative you are, or how organized, or how logical. Nightmares could highlight your fears or reflect the fears of the world around you.

Then again, there are also prophetic nightmares, like seeing yourself hit in the head by a stray baseball, and then it happens in real life, wow, what's up with that?

We just don't know, and that's the beauty of it. We cannot be blamed for any errors of judgment we have in our dreams because it's only our freewheeling subconscious making dubious decisions. For all we know we're shaking something out of our system, and it helps us to resist making similar mistakes while awake. That includes following through on an attraction to a famous movie star.

Sexual fantasizing is its own world, kind of like dreaming. It's hard to pinpoint the source of the images but for average people, they're basically harmless. Because I don't like the idea of checking a box that says "Inappropriate for younger readers," I'll leave it at that.

I will say one more thing about general daydreaming, though. Daydreams can be as fancy as night dreams, where we look into a distant future, we become embarrassingly rich, and are built like athletes who look like models and retire from our sport to become movie-stars.

Night dreaming is still my favorite, though. It's a delightful phenomenon and we're lucky it happens. In our deliciously unpredictable dreams we can feel, see, hear, and smell in abnormal fashions as easily as our senses can appear to behave normally. What will happen next is anybody's guess.

Another bonus is the ability to do whatever we wish and there won't be any penalties. Overeating and drinking too much don't cause problems like they can while we're awake. We can get away with all manner of excesses and wake up without having gained a pound. Enjoy.

Chapter 7: Food and other Styles of Fun

I would just die without food.
– Common Sense

Thank goodness, there is no way we humans can be forced to entirely give up eating. Alcoholics must never drink again, and smokers should never smoke another cigarette if they want to live longer, healthier, and more social lives. TV, Internet, gaming, or social media addictions can be handled by reluctant unplugging, but the one thing our society can never force us to abandon forever is the orgiastic pleasure of food.

Foods are a matter of taste, pun intended. American processed cheese and deep-fried snack cakes might make people from Greenland feel nauseated, but hey, Greenlanders eat blubber. And although I don't eat processed cheese food, if I had to choose I would pick florescent-orange cheese over head cheese. The latter is a European concoction which usually has nothing to do with actual brain matter; it's pretty much made up of jellied flesh from the heads of animals like pigs or cows. I came across head cheese in Canada, where they also eat jellied moose nose. Gag me with a massive nostril.

Favorite foods, let's see. Your tastes might lean toward meat or veggies, sweet, spicy, salty, bitter, sour or savory.[25] You may be one of those people who gets no real thrill from food, but I find that to be discombobulating. If eating is a chore does the person have a favorite food, nonetheless?

---

25 Or "umami." Is that the same as savory? I'm fairly convinced that they're different.

Something simple to prepare and quick to swallow, like hot tea and dry toast?

That still perplexes me. I can understand a love of bread, like soft, steamy croissants or a French baguette with a crispy crust and chewy interior. But toast? Plain white packaged pre-sliced bread with a 2-year shelf-life that one browns in a toaster? I don't get it.

This will come as no surprise to those who know me, but some of my favorite fantasies are about edibles and drinkables. An artfully crafted esoteric cheese, some Kauai Sugarloaf white pineapple, a warm artesian baguette, and a 1945 Mouton Rothschild. My mouth waters as I sit here.

Ironically, bread, cheese, wine, and fruit is also the classic every-person's most delectable meal. I'll have a downgraded version tonight, with extra-sharp cheddar chunk cheese, giant black cherries (on sale yesterday), a small round Italian loaf that I'll bake myself, and an impertinent little Argentinian Malbec (I won't name the vintner because they charge so little for their wines. I can't afford for them to become aware of how easily they could quadruple their profits).

My love of food influences my severe dental phobia. It would be catastrophic for me to be the victim of any condition that would restrict my ability to eat any food. American, British, German, Chinese, Japanese, French, Greek, Jewish, Mexican, Canadian, Italian, and on and on, I am a fervent foodie. Don't get me started about cheese. It's like potatoes or eggs, where the recipe possibilities number in the thousands.

Part of the fun of food for me is preparing it. I cook with pleasure whether or not anyone else will be joining me. I've been asked, "How can you go through that much trouble for just yourself?" My response is often a question, "Do you think you're not worth the trouble?"

Myth of Normal

Say it takes a half hour to make a meal for you and one other. The time is spent pulling out a pot, a pan, a knife, getting veggies and meat from the fridge, cutting and cooking, washing up afterward. Whether there are two people or one, those actions require a similar amount of time. Very little additional time and effort comes from adding a second person, because you only need to chop a bit more on the veggies and clean an extra plate.

This is why I'm baffled by the idea that it's worth it to cook nice meals for two or more, but not for one. Interest in preparing a delicious meal is part of the entire food experience, and I think it helps to keep a healthy weight, too.

The way I work it out in my head is a combination of adding activity—by which I mean cooking—to the eating process, and there's a deeper appreciation of the food because you have lovingly created it. The activity helps to burn a couple of calories, and the appreciation imbues each bite with a specialness that forestalls gluttony.

The same is true of savoring the tastes that can be found in alcohol, particularly wine. Oenophiles[26] purchase their wines with care, they take steps to remove the cork without leaving crumbs in the bottle. They study the appearance of the wine as they swirl it in the glass. They dip their noses over the rim and comb their brains for unique words to describe aromas, be they bold or subtle. It's only after they've examined every nuance that they take a sip, and then they put all the information together and glory in what are hopefully luxuriously delectable flavors.

It takes a lot longer to get an over-the-top, bacchanalian,

---

[26] That's a word for wine lovers. It never crossed my mind that it could sound sinister until I heard a man say it in a family park, and a few nearby mothers nervously tucked their children behind their skirts.

alcoholic buzz if every sip is an absorbing procedure. Moderation occurs more naturally if one eats and drinks for detailed pleasures such as scents and textures.

When it comes to food, I recommend taking time to choose mouth-watering ingredients and put them together in a wonderful way, breathe in the variety of odors while cooking, and "plate" your meal to give it an enticing visual presentation. When you take a bite, think about the way it feels in your mouth,[27] concentrate on the subtleties of what you're tasting. Is there an herb or spice that will brighten or subdue the flavors?

Each bite, each sip, ah yes. When we become involved in the entirety of the experience we don't need to gulp down quite as much as we thought we needed. And the variety we have in First World countries, it is staggering. Even the poorest Americans have access to fruits and sweets and meats and sauces that only the wealthiest kings and pharaohs had available, back in their day. Imagine how King Tut would have responded to chocolate![28]

Another approach to both food and wine is to build anticipation. That's a driving force, like the excitement of planning for a wedding or vacation. Isn't it marvelous to have something to look forward to? It's a lot of fun to plan on investing in a bottle of wine or champagne for a future occasion, and it intensifies the taste of filet mignon or an artisan cheese pizza if we think about it for a few weeks before we indulge.

Everything I've described above sounds abnormally enthusiastic, I think. Yet it's more bizarre to have a dislike for food, which would be like feeling vexed by breathing.

Does the average person eat more fast food or junk

---

27 Unless it's jellied moose nose
28 Chocolate is a Mayan discovery, long after Tut was alive.

Myth of Normal

food than healthy food? I have no idea. (I should note that I put foods with minimal ingredients into the "healthy" category, and that includes natural ice creams, cheeses, pastas, salsas, and so forth. In my mind, preservatives don't belong in natural foods.) If average American diets are so dangerous, how do we keep increasing our population? Maybe our bodies can become accustomed to unnatural foods.

Eating so much or so little that it causes health problems is not what regular people do, and the same is true of drinking alcohol. Most humans do not overeat or drink too much. That I do know, but I'm basing it on the world population. My reasoning is that there's a high percentage of people who are so low-income that they cannot afford to eat and drink too much.

I'm still looking for "normal," here... It isn't the norm to eat healthful foods all the time, nor is it normal to binge. I think the closest we can come is that a majority of citizens in First World countries diet often, which again, doesn't work for a global average. As educated rumor has it, 85% of the world's population lives in developing countries.

For approximately a zillion years, the English word "diet" meant eating habits, not losing weight. There have been eras and cultures where thinness was the fad, while in other times and places a heavy body carried more societal weight, as it were. You may be one of the fortunate few whose size and shape matches today's fashion, but odds are, you're not.

So many of us torture ourselves with trying to fit into the right clothes or the most insistent expectations. What a struggle, it causes frustration and a discomfiting sensation of defeat. But if you look at the people who were depicted as exceptionally attractive in history, no matter what their size,[29] their comfort with themselves is evident. They look sensual

---

29 "Rubenesque" is a great example

and sexy through the eyes of the artists, and it emerges on the canvas.

When you're okay with how you look, your body size is irrelevant. Otherwise, there's enough information out there about foods that can kill us, and if you're not sure your doctor (or Dr. Internet) can fill you in. In the meantime, remember that the only real thing that's average about you is an inability to lock into a specific appearance for the rest of your life.

Better to be content with your natural self.

Chapter 8: Hello Gorgeous[30]

Loving yourself isn't vanity.
It is sanity.
- Katrina Mayer

Fine, wavering lines separate modesty and flamboyance. Egomaniacs are annoyingly flagrant, but shy people are often missed in a crowd. Embedded in the layers of those extremes are people who have authentic self-respect but are accused of narcissism, while on the other side are those who sneakily gaze into every reflective surface, but pretend their appearance is meaningless.

The rest of us are somewhere in between, chancing it with happenin' hair one day and spinach-teeth the next.

Appearance is a big one. The worst situation of all is to worry that you're not attractive, but you'd be surprised by how gorgeous you are. I mean it. All that's left is for you to believe it's true.

A hypothetical situation would work here, even though that approach gets a bad rap. I'm not sure why. Maybe it's from law shows and martial arguments, when an indignant accuser says, "I will *not* deal in hypotheticals!" Personally, I love hypothetical analogies because they engage the imagination. "What if?" is such an inspiring question!

I'll venture to say that people who buy lottery tickets know how unlikely it is they'll win, but they're willing to pay a few bucks for hypothetical scenarios of "What if I win?" It's a

---

30 When I first heard Barbara Streisand say that in Funny Girl (1968), I thought (to the effect of), "You go, Girl."

small investment in self-generated entertainment.

In any event, I'll offer an imaginary situation now.

Say you're a shy person and you want to ask a coworker on a date. You decide to use a text for the request, but you're so nervous that you add a caveat to your decision, avoiding discussion and leaving it to the other person to show up or not: "If you want to have coffee with me I'll be at the Main Street Cafe tomorrow, 6pm. Hope to see you there." You send the text before you can change your mind.

Now the waiting begins.

Did I mention that you sent the text at 10am? Your hoped-for date would be 6pm tomorrow, which means it'll be 20 hours before you find out whether the person will show up.

You get wrapped up in waiting for the day to arrive, obsessing on details like, "Why did I add that final sentence? It was saying, 'Don't bother texting back, just show up or not.' If I hadn't added that, I might have heard a response right away. Now I have to wait and hope for the best."

As time keeps ticking, the obsession over details finds new avenues. Like, "Did she see me walk past her at lunchtime? Did I look okay?" or "Why did he walk past me today without so much as a smile? Does that mean he won't show up?"

Now that I think about it, I notice that I'm separating out the types of thoughts one might have based on whether they're male or female, but that's a waste of time. It's not necessarily on-track to think the woman's worries would be, "Did Chris notice my new blouse?" and the man's concerns as, "Could Pat tell that I messed up my beard while I was shaving this morning?"

There's no cause to genderize because plenty of men are careful about their clothing choices, and women sometimes have an appallingly evident chin-hair. (How could it have

Myth of Normal

grown four inches without her noticing?)

What it comes down to is of all the worries I describe above, none are any more excessive than the stress everyone else experiences. Everybody delves into minutiae to a ridiculous degree.

Also, there are encouraging odds that a person you think you can ask for a date is attracted to you. The most rational way to build up the nerve to ask is because you've probably seen or sensed some signals. Those are odds, not certainties, but if the attraction does exist, she or he is not picking out your clothes or plucking at your chin-hairs for examination. The focus is on what's attractive about the overall you, just as you're drawn to more than surface qualities in that person.

Hopefully. Depends on the type of date you're seeking.[31]

We've all heard about how we're hard on ourselves when it comes to how we look. "My hair is drab, my eyes are too far apart, I'm not comfortable with my neck, chest, hips, and (perhaps most daunting) yikes, what's up with my stomach?"

There's the double-vertical line that first started forming between your eyebrows when you were thirteen, or the visual pain of watching your eyebrows growing into a unibrow by the time you turn sixteen. The very color of your eyes matters—I once heard somebody complain, "My eyes are mud brown" and I thought, "Looks like more of a polished oak, to me."

Perspective.

I know there are a precious few who look into the mirror and see the beauty of a classic god or goddess. Most of us catch every single flaw. The face in the mirror or the body below, look at that mole, the scar, check out the small hands,

---

31 Booty-call (surface) or lifemate (depth).

or feet so big we don't know why people aren't leaving clown shoes on the porch during Halloween.

The cells we're born with can make for some unusual bodies. The person isn't abnormal, it's the cells.

Moles and awkward feet and whatever else disturbs you about your appearance, these so-called flaws add character. You're seeing yourself in a way that others aren't. Yes, there are many photos and video recordings we can use these days to get a better sense of how we look outside the mirror, but those pix and vids don't carry your vibe, your unique energy.

The elements of you that make you attractive have little to do with your flaws, and if you can ignore this counterintuitive observation, flaws can also add to your attractiveness.

Is there *anything* that looks good about you? It could be the shape of your mouth or the sweetness others find in your gaze. Where you see a frightful mass of unruly hair, someone else is enraptured by your charming abandon.

Some people are drawn to brilliant minds, or it could be the size of an income that's a big turn-on. I know the attraction of income can be off-putting, but hey, the one who's drawn to you might be thinking about the type of personality required to earn those big bucks.

Charisma, that can really make otherwise plain or unpleasant people seem striking. This point can be clarified by a political example—there will more on politics coming up, please don't close this book now that I've said that. Politics have a lot to do with what's normal or not, and I'll try to be gentle.

Now back to my strand about charisma, and also self-confidence, and how I can illustrate my point about attractiveness. I'll start by asking which of the following politicians are attractive:

Myth of Normal

Abraham Lincoln
John F. Kennedy
Adolf Hitler
Donald Trump
Melania Trump
Either Clinton
Either Obama
Vladimir Putin

While reviewing that list you probably saw names of people who are appealing to you. I bet you also instinctively know that the ones you think are not so good-looking are attractive to other people.

Abraham Lincoln is attributed with saying, "If I had two faces, would I be wearing this one?" There are many people who found him handsome in an austere kind of way, but he wasn't feeling it. He saw his physical flaws and assessed a lack of handsomeness, but attractiveness is not the same.

"But Hitler?" comes the knee-jerk exclamation. "How could anyone think Hitler was handsome?" Or, "Putin? Really? That weak-chinned rodent?"

Really. I've heard that a lot of Japanese women bought a calendar of Vladimir Putin where he's showing his hairless chest along with his chin-challenged face.[32] Apparently it has something to do with what is perceived as "raw manliness."

That some would find Melania Trump visually displeasing is another confusing revelation, because she was literally a fashion model. Opinions that she's unattractive aren't likely to be associated with her physical features, so it must be connected to her personality, her nationality, her accent, or who knows, maybe it's political.

---

32 David Moye, HuffPost 12/17/2018

R.L. George

Melania married the Don either because she loved him (that's honorable), or because he was a wealthy, famous man (that's mercenary). Some women think wealth is quite enough, but others might find it to be an offensive motivation for marriage. On the other hand, those who see Trump as saturated with Putin-like alpha-male hunkiness would say, "Melania got lucky because he's rich, famous, *and* cute!"

Is Trump attractive to you, dear reader? Even heterosexual men can admit if they think another guy is good-looking. If Trump is ugly to you, does that mean you find/found Bill Clinton and/or Barack Obama attractive?

Yes, I think it does mean that. Personally, I've been able to recognize compelling features in every one of the people I listed, but whether or not I find them *attractive* is based on whose personality I like or dislike.

I remember from all the way back to when I was a kid and learned that Hitler was adored by Nazi women, and yes, they thought he was hunky. It took a while for me to give focus to the word "Nazi" before "women," because all I could think was, "No way. They *pretended* to think he was handsome because otherwise they might be tortured and/or killed."

Yes, I was young enough to believe for moment that a woman could be executed for not drooling over a dictator. Throughout my subsequent adult life I found out how unlikely that is. Now, having gained a modicum of additional wisdom, I'm back to thinking dictators are so freakin' insane that they just might have a woman executed for saying something harsh to a tyrant, like, "Get your slimy hands off me." But that's just cynicism. The reality must lie somewhere in between.

The bottom line returns to perspective. Elements of your personality are wired in such a way as to define what attracts you to people, meaning your political persuasion can

Myth of Normal

influence your taste in appearance. Admirers of Hitler and Putin genuinely saw/see them as visually fetching. I swear to Trump supporters that the Obamas are beguiling to Obama fans, and I promise Obama fans that in the eyes of Trump's followers, he and his wife are knock-outs.

What is it about powerful people, that they can have such a profound effect on half the public, no matter what the other half thinks? Charisma. Self-confidence. It's magnetic, and we must have magnets in our eyes because we see charismatic, self-confident people as resplendently breathtaking.

Now back to the way you think about your own appearance. Although I suspect there are some genetic influences involved in charisma and self-confidence, I also believe those qualities can be learned. That learning process starts with accepting who you are as the perfect representation of you because no one else can do you better.

Yes, I went there, I said you are perfect.

The inimitable perfection of each individual in his or her own self is a societal norm based on uniqueness. You can wear the same fashionable jeans that everyone else is wearing, but it's the way *you* wear them that gives them spunk or sass. One woman can put the fire in smokey-eye makeup, while on another woman it looks like she peered through some gag-binoculars and was left with scary circles. When it comes to the "man-bun," some guys should go for it, while others need to let it go as a fad that will pass, may it rest in peace.

Others may have a nose or a smile like yours, but nobody else has the combination of features and personality quirks that result in the quintessential you. What you have comes from hard work or luck, meaning you either work for those 6-pack abs, or you were born with Angelina Jolie-eyes. What you do with what you've been given, and how your self-work pays off, is your choice.

It's true that there are limits when it comes to some facets of you. For instance, you're stuck with your bone structure unless you can afford some major surgery, and if you're under 5' tall there isn't even an astronomically expensive surgery that can fix it.[33] Once that type of understanding settles in, you can accept that you have the luxury of working with what you've got.

During hard times, like an acne outbreak or lugging an extra 20 pounds around the waist and hips, it's no small solace to say, "So be it, this is me. Here I am, and I will make the best of it." Conversely, it's a burden to think, "Ugh, I'm stuck with who I am and there's nothing I can do with it." Speaking to oneself that way is self-defeating, it's like punching oneself in the face, or tripping oneself while dancing. What fun is that?

Thinking there's nothing you can do to improve who you are is giving in to despair. Making the best of yourself is sparking hope, and hope is better than any drug. It gives you the wings of caffeine and a smoker's nicotine zing, it relaxes remorseless tension, ignites motivation, and inspires the imagination.

It isn't easy to let go of the negative views you have of yourself, but it helps to recognize your flaws as potential benefits. Are you achingly shy or awkwardly funny? Some people are enchanted by those traits. You may spend far too much time drifting into fantasies about faraway places, but you'll catch the eye of an adventurer. Your tendency to obsess over details will make you look like a hottie to someone who's terrified of germs to the point of phobia.

Seeing your flaws as benefits is tricky, but now that you've tried that, you can acknowledge your qualities more

---

[33] Yet.

easily. They could be physical, like flawless posture or a facial structure that every sculptor wants to capture. Or, your best qualities may be in your personality, like scintillating wit or radiant kindness. Your qualities are there somewhere, and you know they're there. Believe in them, accept that you do have attributes that will spark desire, love, and respect in others.

Is it hard for you to admire anything about yourself? That's okay too. It means you'll never been accused of immodesty or narcissism.

You are who you are and once you settle into that, self-confidence can emerge. "How could I be anybody else?" you wisely ask yourself. "Of course I'm me."

I'm convinced that self-confidence translates to your own particular style of charisma. Others may not know where it comes from, but you'll know. It's you doing the perfect you because nobody else could do you better.

You're not normal, thank goodness, and it looks good on you.

R.L. George

Chapter 9: Faith and Politics

*Nobody realizes
that some people
expend tremendous energy
merely to be normal.*
– Albert Camus

I checked a few sources for the definition of a "norm" in order to make sure I had it right, and I was struck by how terse it all sounds. Pedantic descriptors, like, "Official standards" and "governing conduct." There are also directive words, like "doing what's accepted" and "following the expectations" laid out by society. So, in order to be accepted we're expected to behave as society directs, or wishes. Behaving as ourselves is nowhere to be found in the definition of a norm.

Norms are related to national, cultural, religious, and political affiliations. It's said religious norms are what originally set the standards of human rights, but there's some irony there; rights can be skewed (or skewered) by religions that lean more toward describing moral imperatives than encouraging individual liberties.

Religions variously demand that we view dead bodies, wrap the bones in cloth, or burn the dead and consume the ashes.[34] In Spain's Tenerife they hold funeral services for sardines. I had a friend in Mexico who dumped tequila over the grave of a lost buddy each year. Some cultures celebrate death while others mourn the departed for the rest of their

---

34 The last is a Brazilian and Venezuelan custom.

Myth of Normal

lives.

Marriages are different everywhere, too, even within one's own country. Mormons can't invite non-Mormon guests to their temple ceremony, Jews stomp on a glass, and reportedly, Greeks have big fat weddings. Americans have been known for marrying in themed regalia, dressing as Star Trek or Star Wars characters. In some parts of Germany the bride and groom cut a log together.

In Korea the gift of a fowl is sometimes presented to the mother of the bride. I think that has become symbolized with an artistic carving rather than a real bird, but I bet in the old days there were some delicious feasts (or playful pets) being passed around. In Kenya, fathers evidently spit on their daughters,[35] and I've heard that in India the sisters of the bride steal the groom's shoes. Gee, I wonder what that act could signify?

No religious or traditional act is universally preferential or detrimental. As always, it's a matter of perspective. We know that to be true because people of conflicting religions tend to fight, sometimes to the death, in the name of their own beliefs.

Speaking of death, there are many viewpoints of what happens in the afterlife. One might be gifted with eternal bliss, encounter many virgins, or achieve complete enlightenment, but the real bottom line is with regard to the Creator.

A faction or individual may try to convince you that your Creator is not the real one. That's like saying your father isn't really the person who impregnated your mother (although in that case it's usually the mother who's being insulted). In any event, as much as you believe your Creator is the only

---

35 Let's hope that has become symbolic, too, with nothing more than a gesture rather than actual spittle.

legitimate one, the people who disagree with you believe they're right with the same alacrity. They cannot change your mind any more than you can change theirs. What to do?

Acceptance is our best option. I realize some religions don't subscribe to universal acceptance, it isn't good enough because one must worry about the immortal souls of nonbelievers. Yet if you try your level best to convince people and they refuse to convert, all that's left is acceptance that they'll suffer in the afterlife. It would be unbearably painful to blame that on yourself, and holding anger toward the unconverted would be unendurable. Misplaced anger is toxic for you, not for person who is angering you. Feeling endlessly angry at someone or some group adds dark weight to your own energy, which seems to be missing the point entirely. Isn't the religious message of converting others about en*light*ening them? It would be hard to convince people that yours is the best belief if it gives you excessive stress.

Acceptance. That comes up in a famous serenity prayer about changing what we can, and accepting what we can't change. There are exceptions to acceptance, of course, for instance if I were kidnapped I'd like to think I'd never accept it as a forever situation. On the other hand, I'd also like to think that once I escaped, I'd be able to accept the fact that my kidnapper was suffering from a mental illness, and find forgiveness in myself.

A quick aside about forgiveness: I know it can be hard to let go of fury toward someone who has wronged you. Why bother letting go of it? Maybe your bad vibes toward that person can make his or her life miserable, and that could result in a satisfying sensation of revenge.

However. What finally convinced me that forgiveness is the best route is when I realized if not for forgiving—and perhaps more importantly, being forgiven—I would be completely alone in this world.

It is difficult to forgive some of the more profound wrongs against us. How does one even go about moving toward forgiveness, much less arriving there? It comes back to achieving a measure of self-serenity in your lifetime, and accepting that others commit wrongs and make mistakes.

Acceptance is a big piece of the serenity puzzle, and I think it should extend to more than just religious and psychological ideals about well-being. Politics are a prime example. The split in opinions is always drastic, no matter where you live, with each side shuddering at the ugliness of the other while melting in the glorious glow of their own political savvy.

Should there come a time when you learn your political choice has become an embarrassment, I still think you're only partially wrong. As everyone knows, about half of American citizens usually shun whichever president is in office. If after years of gaining wisdom you change your mind about who's best to lead, it's little more than shifting from one foot to the other. About half the country is going to agree with you at any given moment in the history of our governments.

I'm not backing that up with statistics for the reasons I described near the start of this book. It's obvious that we don't each have an intractable political belief that's fully unique, because if that were true, it would be too hard to group together as a nation. We find a way to bend, rarely standing stock-still in a single position.

We learn how to group together through cultural influences but religion and politics continue to give us stern commands. Those last two are very different phenomena but they're interwoven. Do religions have more impact on norms than governments? Maybe, because governments follow religious tenets like, "Thou shalt not kill."

Then again, governments could have a greater impact on establishing overall norms because they have a longer list of infractions to deal with. I'd bet a whole nickel that there's nothing about jaywalking in any religious texts.

Yes, I believe governments and their laws direct our behaviors more intimately, and they follow through on punishment in real-time rather than in an afterlife.

The "national" element of secular norms is reflected by government, but which is stronger, the people or their leaders? When a new nation is formed it's because people are steering political vehicles, but the resulting government then becomes the driver. It's pretty cockeyed when you think about it.

Say a king declares, "From this moment on, the word 'consarnit' is officially stricken from spoken language! Punishment for its use will be thirty days of silence." Now the word is stuck in his head when he says, "As of this moment, everyone must now stop complaining about that wretched word. I mean what I say, consarnit!"

Everyone heard the decree and the subsequent transgression, so the king must remain silent for thirty days. If he doesn't, he'll set a bad example. So he closes his mouth and sure enough, some sneaky jester posing as a representative of the king can take advantage of the situation. "Everybody should assume that until the king says otherwise, we can have a party in the castle! Speak aloud now, o king, if you wish us to desist!"

Seriously, kings and dictators expect us to believe they're divine, but they're as human as every one of us. They have slips of tongues and errors in judgment. Their charisma and self-confidence attracts some but it's off-putting to others. This is life as a human being.

One of the ideas I'm trying to float is that the most noteworthy politicians are abnormal. They're kinder or meaner than all who came before them, they're more calming or disturbing, they're too hawkish or dovish—they're too much of one thing or not enough of another. They're excessive personalities, not average. The people who are the most memorable leaders of countries are the deviants.

All that said, the interactions between nations, as well as the external and internal politics and religions of nations, they're in a constant sway due to cultures. I see it as a kind of perpetual motion machine, where religions sprout cultures (for or against theologies), cultures create nations, nations establish politics, and governments (made up of individuals) set down laws and codes of ethics.

We're all together in this, whether we realize it or not. The sad news is there are always entities that can make us feel outside the loop. It could come from the top, landing you in prison because you don't agree with a law or religious tenet. Or, it may be that the media, in a reflection of popular culture, makes you feel like an outcast. I'm not sure if it's worse to be persecuted by your peers or your leaders, but many would agree the latter is the most dangerous. They have the most power, which is puzzling because they're outnumbered by citizens.

Monarchies and dynasties are classic, with all the regalia and assumptions of royal lineages, but people have risen up against them with, for example, guillotines.[36] Oligarchies are comprised of the elite, and they keep secrets from their citizens as much as every other government. Some think they see oligarchies everywhere, because the elites have the most money, don't they? Not necessarily. Governments that are run by its wealthiest citizens are called "plutocracies." In a

---

[36] e.g. England's King Charles I, France's King Louis XVI, and who can forget Marie Antoinette?

plutocracy the ones in charge aren't necessarily personally rich, but if not, they're easily bought by those who are.

Democracies are not into beheadings, and they do make attempts to shed light on what's going on in the country and in the world. However, as we've learned in the States, lobbyists represent those who are fantastically wealthy and buy votes for their masters. It can draw a sigh from those of us who are regular citizens, but our government does represent *us*. We vote for the people who are purchased by lobbyists, and by our vote, we indicate approval of the interests represented by wealthy people and organizations that purchase influence.

Which government would be best for everyone is and always will be the subject of international debate. Is there a specific type you would choose, dear reader, if you were allowed to choose? Is it a good idea to be the subjects of a king or queen? Are rich people the best faction to run countries?

We Americans make our choices and hope that we'll get what we've asked for, but no matter what, at least half the country is up and the other is on a downer. Some say half are clueless and the other half feels misunderstood. It's all such a muddle, the best we can do is vote our true selves and keep our fingers crossed.

The last thing I'll say about religion and politics is as much as it seems that everyone is either all the way conservative or all the way liberal, that's not true. I'm blessed with a number of friends who vote in various ways, meaning left, right, and center. Because these are close friends we talk about everything with refreshing honesty, and over the years, I've learned that no one is truly locked into every position of their religion or political party.

I've known anti-gun pro-life people, which is pretty sensible if one takes "Do not kill" as etched in stone, and I've also known pro-choice gun-owners. There are devoted recyclers who think there's no such thing as global warming. Gays and lesbians can be Catholics and Muslims, conservatives or liberals. There are individuals who go to church fairly often but don't actually believe in God, and others believe in God but not organized religion.

I know people who were positive that Obama was other-than-American, yet those same people have interracial family members. I know legal immigrants who think illegal immigrants should be drawn and quartered, Mexicans who dislike African Americans and vice-versa, powerful women who are in love with misogynists, and rich people who believe in socialism. The list goes on and on.

We humans belong to larger groups, but this does not mean one specific group automatically does all our thinking. If you're concerned about how different you are from those in your family, country, prayer circle, or political party, I hope you can breathe a sigh of relief knowing that everyone else has a position as unique as yours.

R.L. George

Chapter 10: You Against the World

> *I occasionally think how quickly our differences worldwide would vanish if we were facing an alien threat from outside this world.*
> – Ronald Reagan

What I've said about religions and governments is not restricted to the United States, of course not. Spiritual and political beliefs have countless layers within every state, province, and culture on this planet. It's like peeling back an onion and finding another full onion at the center. That innermost nugget of complexity is us, the individuals. Each on our own, we're as multifaceted as the planet Earth and all its nations.

We have layers within ourselves because we grow new skins throughout various phases of our lives without shedding the old. This is why we get it, we understand what's said by our culture, family, etc., but we rarely go along with every bit of it. Our independence asserts itself, inevitably, one way or another.

An example: someone who's raised to think Americans are finks may be uncomfortable with a witty New Yorker, a boisterously friendly Texan, a sweet Nebraskan, or a laid-back Californian. However, given time, that non-American will find likable personalities somewhere in that mix. Americans are as diverse as Europeans, East Indians, and Chinese.[37] Countries

---

37 Speaking of diversity... U.S. and U.K. accents can be hard to understand sometimes, but there are HUNDREDS of Chinese dialects! Surely they have different accents, too. How interesting their communication must be.

Myth of Normal

are made up of individuals who are likable or not, despite their national identity.

Americans are sophisticated enough to make astute observations about citizens of other countries, yet naturally we're nervous about those who are seen as enemies during a given era. We're raised or schooled by our families and cultures, who convince us that "others" are right or wrong, for us or agin' us. We believe what we're told until experience illuminates some finer details.

This is stating the obvious, but we cannot know the truth about an individual personality until we meet that individual. Listen to the angst in the voice of a person who proclaims, "You don't know me!"

Governments try to get under our many layers of skin, they hope to inscribe ideas on all levels of self that we're expected to build up throughout our lives. They start with early messages of guidance and then ease into later life lessons. National leaders work around the influences of childhood and grown-up life in order to group us together around issues. They say what they must to appease the citizenry, which is not to say we'll do what they've said.

There are plenty of reasons for governments to pull us together as a nation. It's natural to love one's own country, and our nations need us to be patriotic in case we must be called upon to defend our homes. It's a symbiotic relationship, because of course your home has deep meaning for you, and your leaders want you to defend it.

Home. The physical surroundings of the place will seep into our cells, whether we grew up with awesome mountain vistas or coastal living with its scent of an ocean, sea, or gulf. The desert has its own style of beauty, and the same is true of cityscapes.

Beyond the physical location is the sensation, or

essence of home. Family, security, treasured possessions. National leaders rely on our love of home, and they guide our thinking about defending our way of life as best as they can. And yes, one approach is to turn citizens against people from other cultures. They speak the word "others" with dark foreboding.

We seem so different from those who are unlike us in facial characteristics, skin-tone, language, and upbringing. But unless we find a way to live (not visit, but live) in a number of countries, we have no choice but to rely on what we hear in the media, on the Internet, and so forth. Hearsay.

I'm a fan of free press, but on the other hand, I wish we could have a more rounded version of what the media says about citizens of countries that aren't their own. It is not helpful to define individuals by listening to talking heads or the news-choosers who pick each day's spin.

When we ignore propaganda we think for ourselves, and we deserve that right. Unfortunately, it's only easy to ignore propaganda that disagrees with our own thinking. The real challenge is to set aside preconceptions even though we're hearing, "Hey, *you're* right, and the other people are wrong!" That's the hook. They get our attention with, "You're right!" and then start manipulating our future ideas. We become easy-pickins for those who wish to do our thinking for us.

Our ideas are fine as they are, and they occur even while our thoughts are manipulated—internally and externally—every minute. We're confronted by a personal catastrophe or epiphany and everything is colored by different shades of understanding. Also movies, sitcoms, music, art, it's all capable of readjusting our perspective. It happens in school and at work, while we're having a conversation out on the street or at home reading a book (i.e. fiction, or something like this).

Your opinions matter to me. If you have strong

agreement or opposition to anything I'm saying in these pages, I wish we could sit and discuss over coffee or wine. Strange as it sounds, I'm hoping that you're reading this because you have something to say about it. In my fantasy, you've picked up this book with its unabashedly cynical title because it made you think about your own ideas on the topic. "Will the author agree with me or present some rational argument against my position?"

Yes. Ideally—perhaps paradoxically—both. But when it comes down to the final decision, you're right. Your opinions are correct because they belong to *you.*

Someone would have every reason to say, "Wait a minute."

I wait.

"What if," Someone continues, "I think everyone else should agree with me?"

It's fine to think that.

"What if," Someone persists, "they don't agree with me?"

Immanuel Kant pops into the conversation. "Why not change your mind and agree with *them*?"

Someone: "There's no reason I should."

Kant: "If you maintain that you should not change your mind, you're setting a precedent that no mind should be changed upon demand. That includes *them* refusing to change for *you.*"

Someone might walk away from that conversation and all books on the topic because it's perplexing, but Kant called it a "categorical imperative."[38] His point is related to doing unto others. In his theory, our words and/or actions set standards

---

[38] "Act only according to that maxim whereby you can, at the same time, will that it should become a universal law."

about how we think we everyone should else should behave. Or, as Kant puts it, what we think should be a universal law.

I'm reminded of a time that I thought nobody should have to eat liver, ever. I was very young, trapped in front of a cold piece of the leathery organ on my dinner plate. The siblings had gone off to play and the parents were watching TV in the family room. My seat was well within the peripheral vision of my mom, aka "Mombo," but she didn't need to pay close attention because I wouldn't be able to leave my seat without her noticing.

I sat stoically staring at that piece of food, which is offensive to most children under the age of nine. After about a half hour Mombo ambled past for a bathroom break, and although she glanced at the lump on my plate, neither of us made a comment. She returned to the living room with another glance, and I said, "I'm done, can I go out and play?"

"You're not done," she replied.

I showed her my empty plate.

My tall, imposing Mombo strode over like Beatrice Arthur[39] and demanded, "Where is it?" (like Maude).[40]

"I ate it."

"I just walked past and you had the whole piece. You took one bite an hour ago and now you've wolfed down the rest in a matter of four minutes?"

"Yes, I ate it."

Mombo looked under the table and inside my mouth and turned a slow circle to examine my surroundings, but there was no place I could have tossed or hidden the liver. I kept

---

39 Dorothy on the show "Golden Girls."
40 Bea was also on a show called "Maude." Surely everybody knows Bea Arthur because there are hundreds of thousands, perhaps millions of Internet and cable and satellite channels, and at least one of them shows her old shows.

insisting I had eaten it all. Mombo said, "You're lying, I don't know what you did with it but you're lying and for that, you get a swat on the bottom." She pulled me up from my seat to swat me, and there it was, stuck to my backside.

My mother had a great sense of humor but she was so astonished by discovering my ruse—she almost slapped the liver before her brain caught up with what her eyes were seeing—instead she peeled it off, flopped it onto my plate, and ordered: "*Finish it!*"

I never did take another bite. Mombo left me sitting there for another interminable amount of time, allowing me to believe that I had no choice but to chow down, but of course she didn't expect me to eat bottom-liver. Rest her soul, I'm sure she's giggling from the great beyond as I write this.

That story is aligned with Kant's categorical imperative. His arguments are often directly related to breaking rules and lying. By sitting on my liver I was willing it to be true that no child should have to eat yucky-tasting food, and I stand by that, but I should not have lied to make my point. My punishment would have been no different if I had said, "I cannot, will not, shall not eat that liver. It will sicken me from my tastebuds to my bowels."

Incidentally, I asked Mombo years later, "Why did you insist we kids eat foods that we found so disgusting? There were other affordable options that had the same vitamins, and they would have tasted much better."

Her response was to the effect of, "I know, isn't that crazy? When I look back on it I can see how unnecessarily pushy it was, but it was just the done thing. Parents made kids eat liver and Brussels sprouts and stinky fish, and when the children complained, they were told about starving children in other countries. Your kids weren't allowed to leave the table until they finished their meal, or their little butts were paddled."

Following the done thing does have downsides. Some say kids are getting far too many desserts and far too little paddling, these days, such are our current mores. I don't think we can judge the results of our modern way of life until we see what our children do with *their* children.

Even if I did have an opinion about which generation does it best, I remain reluctant to suggest that others agree with me. By believing people should change their way of thinking to mine, the implication is that I should also change my way of thinking to theirs. It's this type of conundrum that makes me return, always, to acceptance.

Accept that your ideas will differ from others, and although intelligent debate can persuade adjustments in thinking, we cannot force—or be forced to—change on demand. Accepting this truth is what can help us to stop warring with one another.

The quote I used to open this chapter has a tongue-in-cheek quality for me, but I think it captures the essence of seeing each other as potential enemies until another enemy unites us. Borders would dissolve against an alien attack, and everyone judged "human" would pass muster, regardless of differences that are glaring right now. There's enormous power in unity. Alien attackers would lose against a unified Earth.

One of the great things we have in common is a thread woven through each of us, and that thread is our typical ability to be abnormal. At the instant we embrace our individualism, we can dismiss all the software because our hard drive kicks in and says, "This calls for a whole new way of thinking."

By software I mean the input that surrounds us every day, influencing our thoughts. While we're alone we get to indulge in our *own* thoughts. It is true that whether we're with

Myth of Normal

others or by ourselves will affect our thinking, but it also directs our behaviors. Is that a good thing? Let's see...

R.L. George

Chapter 11: Alone and Together

> *I only go out*
> *to get me a fresh appetite*
> *for being alone.*
> – Lord Byron

If I knew a passing neighbor would be able to glance into my windows and witness me dancing to the theme song of "Spongebob Squarepants," I would surely rethink doing so. Rethinking it doesn't mean I wouldn't do it, but if I did, I would try to publicly balance it with something more mature, like raking the leaves in my yard. We can't help but remain aware of our public versus private persona, what matters is how much we care about the opinions of others. Apparently, I cotton to the idea of others knowing I can be both playful and hard-working. Yet I'm not an exhibitionist, and would prefer that peekers and peepers stay away from my windows.

Collectivist cultures don't value being alone as much as individualist cultures do. That could explain why the concept of behaving with others as you would alone, and vice-versa, is founded in an Asian philosophy. Those who are rarely alone have a lot more practice with sustaining consistent behaviors.

I wonder how comfortable one can be knowing there's always someone lurking behind a closed door, in an adjacent room, or on the viewer's side of a camera. Presumably, those who were born and raised in collectivist cultures have better practice with a constant lack of privacy.

Here in the 21st century, a lens is directed at you while you're waiting in a subway, pulling into a parking lot, or walking through a grocery store. Crime shows and movies illustrate the

Myth of Normal

modern ability to track criminals with well-placed street cameras and satellite surveillance, and totally innocent couples have been caught coupling by drones.

Oops, I've just talked myself through a stream of thought that started with wondering what it would be like to never be truly alone, and ended with technology's invasion on privacy. It sounds like the plot of a sci-fi novel from the 1940s, where everything you do—and think!—is observed, evaluated, and redirected.[41]

It isn't a bad idea to behave alone as you would in public, because as you read this, your actions are one click away from YouTube. But what bothers me about the suggestion of consciously, continually measuring our behaviors is that we ought to be able to let loose on our own time.

On the other hand, looking at it from the outside in, we'd have harried spouses yelling at each other in movie theaters, beat-deaf motorists honking along with their favorite song, and nudists in restaurants saying, "But this is how we relax at home!"

So, adapting to public propriety isn't a bad idea, but by definition, it shouldn't have to apply at home. It's like the difference between and indoor and outdoor voices. When we're running through nature we can let our voices fly, and save moderation for enclosed spaces.

Do you sing while you're alone? If so, I applaud you. Singing is one of those types of art that everybody can do it, even if some are renowned only for their shower-stall and stuck-in-traffic solos. If love is the balm of the soul, singing is the lubricant of the spirit.

How about talking to yourself? I don't know who first

---

41 George Orwell's *1984* is a popular example. A prescient book, considering that it was published in 1949.

associated talking to oneself with some kind of psychological pathology. You may not remember this far back, but talking to yourself starts happening as soon as you can speak.

The infant who says, "Bah-ma-buh-da," or the two-year-old who sees a prickly bush and says, although no one is paying attention, "Owie." Or there's the three-year-old who looks at a toy his brother had been playing with and whispers, "Mine."

Then there are times like my liver vignette, when you might have been nine or ten and you've been abandoned to your unfinished meal alone at the dinner table. There's any number of mumbled responses to the parent's command that you will not leave your seat until that plate is clean. (It would not have been beyond my youthful self to engage in a private argument that although I understood the implication, it would be illogical to "clean" a plate if I was not allowed to leave my seat to wash it.)

In any case, odds are good that one would sit there saying, mantra-like, "This sucks" even though everyone else had gone on about their evening, and no one was listening.

I see nothing wrong with talking to yourself. Well, I should say talking *aloud* to yourself. We all have an ongoing internal dialogue, whether it's adding the month's bills, figuring out how to ask for a raise, or pep-talking an approach to a confrontation.

If the idea of being caught talking to yourself bothers you, there are ways to circumvent the potential embarrassment of being overheard by someone in the next room, or by a camera mounted over the bank machine, or by a passing drone.

First, try learning a second language. That way you can practice phrases while you're hunting for your car keys, considering employment possibilities, or wondering what your sneaky neighbor is up to. Not only do you get lots of practice speaking a new language, your sneaky neighbor won't know what you've said about him if he overhears you. When you're cussing about his nosiness in French, Spanish, or one of 200-plus Chinese dialects, he'll think you're just practicing for a trip to a foreign country.

Learning a second language might hold no thrill for you, but there must be something that would enable you to talk to yourself with without shame. Let's see... Maybe you could buy electric earrings? I've seen them, they're made with **LED** lights that wink and glitter. That way, if others see you talking while you're walking down the street alone, they'll assume you're on a Bluetooth.

I'm starting to kid around now, trying to lighten the mood about the ridiculousness of worrying about how others see you as you are when you're alone. Picture someone standing outside your screen door, she's overhearing you talk to yourself. Although she's alone, she's muttering, "Listen to that. He said, 'Where are those wretched car keys?' and then he said, 'Oh, here they are.' He's talking to himself *and* answering himself. Would I ever do that? No way!"

We may as well do what we're doing with at least a modicum of abandon, because it's too taxing to be at the ready every moment of our lives. Somebody is bound to notice us muttering or grumbling, or they'll walk in while we're dancing to a cartoon theme song. At any given time, someone will catch you when you're not wearing your proper face for a given occasion.

Masks and alternate personas do have their place. You and your spouse may have fun shouting at each other, or yes you do prefer eating meals in the buff, but it's important to show some restraint while out in the world. A number of private behaviors are unlikely to initiate new friendships. In public spaces, we need to gradually grow on each other.

R.L. George

There are serious differences between talking to your boss or your spouse, your child or your colleague, in public or private. The distinctions between the self in public versus solitude are reasonable. Yet I will make one more case for being the essentially the same person at all times—as best as one can.

There are instances where we find ourselves wearing an unnecessary mask in social settings, especially when dating someone new, because we want to make a good impression. That's a bad habit, though, because it can be used as an improper excuse when things don't work out. "I wasn't really being myself, that's why she dumped me."

It isn't easy to trust that you can be lovable as-is. If you as yourself gets kicked to the curb it's on you, full stop.

Sure, you'd rather be settled in a relationship, but if you're still only dating it may be because your masks are visible. You also might see masks on others, and *you're* the one breaking it off before it gets too deep. Wouldn't you prefer to be with someone you can really know? The same is true of someone preferring to know the real you, if the two of you are dating. Dating is used for discovery, not deception.

Different faces are necessary in certain situations, such as the workplace versus the home-space, but they shouldn't be something to hide behind. It's like wearing one of those old plastic masks on Halloween instead of painting your skin. The plastic mask totally covers your countenance and casts shadows over your eyes. A creatively painted face reveals your personality, it doesn't hide your features, and your eyes are clear. *You* are still present.

The surveillance techniques of the 21st century are what started me on this path of privacy versus public persona. These days you know you're being watched. There's a camera in your phone, laptop, and your Kindle. I noticed a friend had electrical tape over her laptop camera and I asked, "What about your cellphone?" This very intelligent woman pressed her palm to her forehead in frustration. "It never occurred to me."

I recently saw a commercial about a car that tracks the eye-movement of the driver to ensure that the focus remains on the road. Who's tracking the car that's tracking your very *eyes?*

We all know now that there are chips in cellphones and new cars that transmit your location. Bash your phone to bits and you can be picked up at your latest location with drones. Hide in the attic or basement and you're still not safe from nanobots that look like flies. Pets have implants, and medical procedures like hip replacements are now chip'd with trackable technology. People walk around with pacemakers that are connected to the Cloud.

It's also possible that our flat-screen TVs have pre-installed cameras, ready for the next advances in home entertainment. Our viewing pleasures will someday be meshed with new communication techniques. You'll be binge-watching a show with a bowl of popcorn in your lap and a fifth of tequila by your side, and someone else is watching you watch. "See how his eyes widened with pleasure at the moment the killing occurred in the movie. Maybe our viewer is a murderer himself! Looks like we'll need to watch him more closely..."

Who knows what's next. There are already people who actively encourage voyeurism. To the best of my understanding, the Kardashian phenomenon is based on the fact that their family is watched. They're not acting, they're being as they are, as far as that's possible with the red glow of a recording light in your peripheral vision. The presumption is that viewers are seeing genuine lives, and the impression is that those lives are the same whether the cameras are rolling or not.

R.L. George

    I think the Kardashians do come close to that, given that particularly embarrassing moments can be edited out before public airing. Their publicized lives of sharing time with one another is probably fairly close to how they behave when they're all alone. I would go so far as to say it's also possible for *you* to be the same you in many settings, although you may wonder why anyone would want to watch you. That's anybody's guess, but watch they do. The question is not whether you're being observed, but why. Seriously, someone could be keeping track of you now, as you read these words. Why?

    The immediate supposition is that people want to make money selling you things, and by watching you, they can figure out how to separate you from your cash. There are other reasons, though, that are worrisome.

    I once had an unsettling episode arise and to this day, I've never understood what was going on. What happened is I sent a fiction novel draft through the mail to my editor, I lived in Canada and she lived in Colorado. My book was held up at the border for two months!

    After the first few weeks I called the post office customs department, and the woman I spoke with did some research while I was on the phone. "It is here," she said, "but I can't figure out why it isn't being delivered." I could practically hear her scratching her head. She hunted for answers a bit longer and then said she would have to call me back in a day or two. This woman was very friendly.

    A week passed and I didn't hear from her, so I called her again. When I identified myself her voice changed from its friendliness in our earlier conversation. Now it was flat and overly professional. I asked about my book and she said, "It will be sent on when it is ready to be sent on."

    "Why is it being held up?"

Myth of Normal

She repeated, "It will be sent on when it is ready to be sent on."

"It's a fiction novel," I said. "If I had to pick a genre, the closest would be science fiction. How could it possibly be of interest to the government?"

Automaton voice: "It will be sent on when it is ready to be sent on."

Cue Twilight Zone music. Had I accidentally stumbled upon a realistic trend in my sci-fi book? It's set about 40 years in the future, and the characters often look back on our present day with the clarity of hindsight. My imaginary characters did see some fictionally spooky occurrences going on at the end of the 20th century, but did I pose accidentally accurate guesses about was happening in the real world?

I guess we'll have to wait until 2060 to find out what was really going on from the 1990s to the early 2000s.

What gobsmacked me was why some official saw a manuscript in the mail and thought, "I should open this and read it." I'm sure the holdup had nothing to do with my editor, a fine person. It must have been me, but I'm one writer among hundreds of zillions of international scribes. Why me?

I'm sure that sounds paranoid, but then something similar happened a few years later. Ya can't make this up. I had been contracted to write a memoir for a client who had been the first person to drive a private car all the way around the Mediterranean. The story took place in the 1950s, so of course he was an older gentleman at the time I researched his story.

He'd kept a journal during his journey, and we honed various details by making sure the geography was all correct, we rechecked historical markers, looked into which foods were popular in which Mediterranean countries in the 1950s, that sort of thing. My research required deep explorations of places like Syria, Turkey, and Saudi Arabia.

This was post-911.

One day I signed into the email account I had been using during my research, and instead of my inbox, an unusual message came onto my screen. It said to the effect of, "This account cannot be accessed until further notice." Not, "Sorry, connection problems," or "Temporary upgrade is interrupting email services, please try again later." No, this was personal. The account was under review, and the only reason was because I had been looking into Middle Eastern countries. Yes, it was historical research, but still. People were understandably antsy right after 9/11.

Again, it took months before I could get back into my email account. The novel I spoke of first, the sci-fi, is a long one, and it might take someone a few months to read it. The correspondence in my email account was thicker—writers often write long emails—but as was true with the fiction book, the government employees apparently read every. single. word.

That second experience is more comprehensible because there are algorithms that check for Middle Eastern searches that might somehow be connected to terrorism.[42] Now, decades since the time I wrote that memoir, overall surveillance of Americans has intensified. For example, you have a chat on the phone with a friend about getting new carpeting, and soon after, you'll find an ad in your email account for carpet sales.[43]

I do understand the reasons for overeager surveillance invasions. And I realize it's all compounded by marketing

---

42 Including that word makes me wonder if *this* book will be held up!

43 That sort of thing really does happen, if not to you, ask around and see if others have stories about it. Don't use technology to ask, thought, or you'll find an email ad that tries to sell you books about conspiracy theories.

corporations that take advantage of the information that's gathered. Businesses that target consumers are probably sharing the costs of all the official scrutiny. They're all wading through consumer lives, screening phone calls and emails for bad guys and good sales.

It can't matter if you're behaving differently in public or private situations and locations. Whatever you're doing it's actively being tracked. Or, it's all out there for casual viewing because some passing pedestrians caught you with their cellphones, and they've posted you online. The sad news is that privacy is a thing of the past. The better news is if you've been doing something peculiar and you hope nobody notices, you'll know it can't be too bad if it hasn't shown up on YouTube.

Yet.

R.L. George

Chapter 12: Crime, Guilt, and Punishment

> *We don't seem able to check crime, so why not legalize it and then tax it out of business?*
> – Will Rogers

The Rogers quote that opens this chapter is funny, but dated. Plenty of crimes have been legalized, such as dealing drugs (if you can watch commercial TV for fifteen minutes without seeing a drug ad, you win a "dodged the magic bullet" prize).

Countless generations of governments have stolen money from their people. Elected leaders have flagrantly padded their own lifestyles by using their influence, and the only reason many of them won the election is because somebody paid a shipload of money for advertising.

Speaking of advertising, is "bait and switch" legal? If not, there oughta be a law. I do know there are penalties for false advertising. And then there's the sheer volume! One minute we're leaning toward a favorite show on TV, straining to hear a quiet declaration of love or a whispered threat, and then "HEY! If you knew about this PRODUCT you would NEVER want to live another DAY without it!"

I have quite literally seen people launch out of their seats at the shock of the shouted commercial. It got so out of control that the FCC had to rule against the practice in 2012, but rule-breakers continue blasting out their messages in disproportionately bombastic volumes, to this very day.[44]

Myth of Normal

Lawbreaking... I've heard that extremely wealthy and powerful people get away with murder when it comes to filing taxes, but I have no personal experience with that. I've also heard that if a poor person wins $1 million in the lottery, about half goes to taxes, but if a rich person wins that same amount in a lottery, they keep every dime. Pretty creepy stuff, that. If I were a lottery commissioner I'd be embarrassed.

There are more ludicrous legal/illegal shenanigans of wealth. What of shell companies, and businesses that illegally cut corners in order to save a few shekels? Worse if cutting corners includes details like disposing of toxic waste. And I will say that if extremely wealthy and powerful people never, ever indulge in insider trading, I'll eat my toque.[45]

Privileged people and organizations break laws and rules all the time, Mr. Will Rogers. I wish your joke could be as whimsical as it sounds, but it's impractical. I'm sad to say I have not seen any high-level criminals getting taxed out of business, which is because they rarely, if ever, pay taxes at all.

Evidently it's typical to break rules and the spirit of laws, so if you've had some transgressions or committed a few peccadillos, I hope you haven't been condemning yourself.

What's the most criminal thing you've ever done? There's a long list aside from cheating on taxes, including speeding, driving under the influence, or saying something so annoying in a national forest that it makes a person slug you.[46]

Most people are guided by their own conscience when

---

44 I immediately begin boycotting whatever product or service is being yellingly advertised. Thank goodness wineries don't use the shouting advertisement technique.

45 During my review of this text I thought I wrote "tongue." A "toque" (with the "o" pronounced the same as in "tool") is a knit cap in Canada.

46 Title 7 USC section 1011(f) and 36 CFR section 261.4(b). I am not making this up.

faced with a question of doing the right thing. It's a sorry state of affairs that this means laws are written for those who will do bad things no matter what. We know that's true because look, there are the laws, and there are the people who break them again and again, no matter what the consequences.

People of conscience won't arbitrarily rob a store or mug someone for a handful of cash, using an excuse like, "I really, really want to bet on the horses." Stealing or plundering can meet immediate needs for a day or so, but is it worth a lifetime of guilt?

Those who will commit crimes for any reason—or for no reason—are devoid of guilt issues. If you're regretful about stealing a box of paperclips from work you can let it go now (unless you work at an office supplies store). It may require a bit more self-berating if you take a box of printer ink, but knowing you've done wrong should hold you back from doing it again.

If you've smuggled out an entire printer to use for your home setup, you may need it to print out a new batch of resumes. Come to think of it, why not grab some glossy photo paper, too? It would work well for printing out a professional-looking mugshot.

Seriously. The more wrong something is, the easier it is to see how wrong it is. Is it okay to try a grape or two at the grocery store? I wouldn't have a problem with it if I were the grocery store owner, but some say it's straight-up stealing.

Is it wrong to take money from a cash register at a grocery store? Of course it is. When something is truly wrong there's no doubt in anybody's mind.

It is not abnormal to taste a grape at a grocery store or go home from work with a few fancy paperclips. You don't need to do jail-time if you drove way over the speed limit last Wednesday. Everybody does these things, so they're societal norms. It's an ethical norm to feel crummy about it, if one has a grain of morality in her psyche.

Here's the rub: societal and ethical norms are in constant flux. First world countries have made some pretty stringent laws about the strangest transgressions. As recently as thirty years ago, charges were brought against a woman in Wisconsin for having an extramarital affair. She could have been fined and imprisoned! Today, it would be seen as absurd to bring that level of punishment for adultery.

Debtor's prisons were once a thing, just ask Charles Dickens. Serious prison time, sometimes life sentences, because you couldn't make the mortgage payments, youch. And smoking marijuana? A hundred years from now, some writer will have to convince people that it really did happen back in the day, teenagers were thrown in jail for inhaling smoke from what is a weed.

In some countries it was once fine for grown men to marry little girls, and if the husband died before his wife, she was expected to throw herself onto the flames of his funeral pyre.[47] How crummy is that, when a 42 year-old man marries a 12 year-old girl, then he dies when he's 70 and she's 40, and she's required to do some deadly penance. Talk about injustice!

Thankfully, times change. Norms change. What is criminal today was acceptable yesterday, and what is acceptable today may be against the law tomorrow.

Here's a gut feeling: if you're reading this book, you are not a criminal. Even if you have been criminal in deeds (possibly large but probably small), you are not one of the "bad guys" at heart. You're a thoughtful, curious person who wants to know more about how we flawed human beings can be,

---

47 It's called "sati" or "suttee."

R.L. George

paradoxically, flawless.
    It's just that we sometimes make mistakes.

Chapter 13: Operator Error

> *A person who never made a mistake*
> *never tried anything new.*
> – Einstein

Sometimes we commit a small faux pas. Other times we mess up big. The one thing we cannot do consistently is avoid making mistakes.

Before beating yourself up about errors in judgment, consider the impact. Did it change the world, or just your little patch of land? Big, huge, massive miscalculations are made by people whose decisions reverberate around their neighborhood, town, city, or state. More influential individuals can harm their whole country. Then there are those whose mistakes can adversely effect the entire world.

Adolf Hitler comes up a lot because, well, he adversely affected the entire world. He incorrectly believed he was the best person to run the planet.

Starting at the beginning, mistakes were committed by others who surrounded Adolf. For instance, his baby-daddy should have kept his pants on. From there we can see how that error in judgment, which would seem personal, reverberated outward like a nuke's deadly radiation.

In the grander scheme, others helped Hitler to make his evil gaffes on a global scale. Those who failed to assassinate him messed up miserably—it would be unforgivable if the attempts hadn't been so noble. I've read about six assassination attempts, and it stuns me that a war can kill so many millions of soldiers and civilians, but no one can take out that one and only creature in charge.

R.L. George

Hitler aside, errors were made before the Titanic sank, and before Pearl Harbor was attacked. There's an old story in Discover Magazine that suggests agriculture is the worst thing that ever happened to the human race.[48] That one is debatable, and worthy of debate.

There are theories about who messed up, and how, in every great mistake. Either way, it's hard to care when experiencing the repercussions in real-time. Understanding is built from reflection; we grow when we look back and learn from what has hurt us.

The most obvious examples are that most adults know better than to drink and drive or have unprotected sex. When they do one or both of those things regardless of their knowledge, they're bound to suffer consequences sooner or later. A lost license. An STD, or an unexpected pregnancy. Mistakes that happen once are learning experiences, but when they happen repeatedly, oh the shame!

I don't mean to throw shade on those who are dealing with addictions, that's an entirely separate discussion. This book is about everyday people using common sense when seeing that certain behaviors prove to be harmful. I will say one thing about victims of addiction, though: the most powerful way they gain clarity and head toward recovery is when they suffer an overwhelming catastrophe.

If you're not addicted to a substance or destructive behavior, there's no need to let it climb to a catastrophic pinnacle. Preparedness is the key, but it's useless without information about looming threats. Knowing the threat of a DUI or STD should be enough, but if it isn't, spending a night in the clink or a day at the doctor can solidify the feel of a learning club whacking you upside the head.

---

48 Jared Diamond, 1987.

Myth of Normal

It isn't a requirement to slog through all the errors that provide teachable moments. I've seen other people suffer as the result of poor decisions, and that was enough to stall my own roll down some fairly steep hills toward the Valley of Blunders. It would be terrifying to be incarcerated! If by the end of my life I have never been institutionalized against my will, I can die gracefully.

I'm relieved to learn from watching others. It would be exhausting to have to make all the mistakes myself.

There is a flip-side in that mishaps have more to offer than their teaching capacity. Penicillin is the most widely known example, with Alexander Fleming's moldy petri dishes accidentally saving millions of lives. Many have also heard of the booboos that turned a spring into a Slinky and weak glue into post-it notes.

The quote that opens this chapter speaks to helpful mistakes. Those who are trying new things are bound to err once in a while, and sometimes those errors work out better than carefully measured endeavors.

In other instances, the problems that arise from a bad idea can change your life forever.

We make choices that are good, bad, or dubious. Sometimes it's because we're trying to follow norms that direct our decisions about what to do, but it only takes a microsecond to figure out where that will go. "*Every*body is doing it, why shouldn't I?" and then Mom starts the litany, "So if *every*body is jumping off a bridge..."[49]

On the other hand, feeling boxed in by expectations can drive us toward actions against—or reactions to—rules that don't match our style.

Those are drivers of our choice-making, where we're

---

49 Did somebody say "bungee jumping"?

either trying to fit in or trying to step out. As Quentin Crisp said, "Fashion is what you adopt when you don't know who you are." Whatever is in fashion, be it clothing styles or general attitudes, is what reveals whether we're leaders, followers, or team-players. When we decide against leading or following or even joining a team, we become (wait for it...) utterly unique.

Motivations for our decisions are grounded in respect for the self, and an example is a combination of the other factors. Say it's the year 1935 (or 2019) and college freshmen are expected to endure dangerous hazing. You're a senior and you think hazing is atrocious, but you know it's expected. Option one is you continue to initiate the activities as a senior in the fraternity, option two is you refuse to engage as a pushback on the practice of hazing, but you do nothing to stop it. Or, you're a sophomore team-player who goes along with what the leaders have proscribed, and abuse the freshmen.

The last option is to act on your feelings. During a fraternity meeting, make a motion to end hazing. If you're voted down, you know you gave it a college try to fight against hazardous norms. From that moment on you stop hazing the freshmen in your fraternity. You're seen as abnormal, and you're okay with that. That's when you've decided for yourself what's right or wrong. You are not influenced by peer-pressure, the era, your gender, or your school.

Some think that hazing makes young men more resilient, agreeing with Nietzsche's notion, "What doesn't kill you makes you stronger." A sound argument could be made that it's quite important for people to be pushed to their limits of endurance, and to learn about rebounding.

Others maintain that hazing is brutal, that's all there is to it, because sometimes, people die.[50]

If a norm feels wrong it's okay to stand against it. When your truth has nothing to do with a norm you're taking responsibility for your own thoughts. That's scary, because as is true with my dating analogy a while back, if you later discover your ideas were wrong you have no one to blame but yourself. A person living his or her truth can never use the excuse, "I was only following orders."

On the other hand, it's empowering when your way of thinking is proved correct. The intoxication of that power is that it has nothing to do with money or influence or intoxicants, for that matter. What's powerful is it's all you, what you and you alone have discovered inside your private self.

Bigger issues can take a long time to be proven right or wrong, though. That's when you need to trust your truths, even when they're against the current flow. Then you need to trust your ability to adapt to new information. Again, sometimes your beliefs are against whatever attitude is fashionable, but it's *your* sentiments that are wrong, or filled with holes. Yet if you're true to the notion of truth, you'll adapt.

It sounds difficult to change your mind about what feels like a core truth. However, to be mistaken about hazing, or whether you can drive safely after drinking, will come hideously clear if someone dies. That's a good thing to bear in mind when considering the dubious opinions of others.

What a notoriously arduous task it is, to change minds about untruths related to culture or upbringing. Examples are one gender or race being less significant than another. To this day, it's commonplace in many cultures to assume women or people of color are inferior. And those of varying gender identities and sexual orientation are seen by some to be freakish.

---

50 It has happened disturbingly often. Wikipedia has quite a list.

R.L. George

Presumably, the individuals on the defective side of those beliefs will eventually adapt as new truths continue to emerge. Like human beings, societies do evolve, even if we tend to move at a sluggish pace.

I'm aware of doing a lot of straddling over right and wrong, good choices and bad decisions. That's because we individuals and our societal baby steps have the ongoing challenge of deciding exactly what *is* right or wrong. And we rarely stay put on the conclusions we've made. Ethics and morality are in a constant flux.

Chapter 14: Ethics and Morality

*You have enemies? Good.
That means you've stood up for something,
sometime in your life.*
— Winston Churchill

I associate ethics with philosophy, and morals with religion. Not everybody makes that distinction. I'd also say ethics can be viewed as a practical application of morals. That's why the Churchill quote opens this chapter, because ethics are about more than knowing or choosing between right and wrong. Ethics can guide us in applying that knowledge and those choices. I know the same can be said for morals, but this is the way my mind works through these particularly dense concepts.

Perhaps the most immediate example of advocating morality but behaving unethically is the Inquisition, which began almost a thousand years ago. It started in Europe, and then slithered through the centuries and across the continent until it reared its ugly head in Spain, where it throttled people from the 1400s to the 1800s.

In few, those who didn't agree with the proscribed religion were tortured and/or killed.[51] An individual could believe in a single deity or even the specifically Christian god, but it still wasn't good enough. Follow the strict tenets of Catholicism or your life will become actual hell.

All that torture and killing, but it still didn't work. Many

---

51 Apparently, the murder method of choice was to burn the disagreeably disagreeing humans.

people held onto their own beliefs and only pretended to convert.

The Church wanted to establish a new morality, which is why the Church has enemies – and according to Churchill, that's because the Church was standing up for something. The rub is in the approach. It's honorable to stand up for what one believes, but "Agree with me or I'll kill you" is as harsh as it gets.

I believe a Catholic who asks for forgiveness after having extramarital sex is moral because he wants to be cleansed of his sin. However, if he does the deed again and gets forgiven again, over and over, he's missing the point. The intention behind an act carries far more impact than the act itself.

That may be confusing after what I've been saying about the intentions of the Inquisition, but it still makes sense. The Church's intention was to create a new morality, which is arguably admirable, but the actions were wrong. In the case of the individual sinner it's the opposite, where the intention to hedge his bets against purgatory is flawed. He wants to have his fun and forgiveness too, but that isn't how it works.

Still, when it comes down to it, the act of having sex isn't in and of itself a sin. Killing due to a disagreement does, on the other hand, sound decidedly sinful.

That raises the next question of ethics. Killing is considered immoral by many religions, but nations and factions get around it. The Bible itself gets around it.[52] Killing in the name of protection is reasonable, but protection from what? Surely it must be something or someone very menacing, like stopping a murderer before he can commit the act. Otherwise it's closing the barn door later with a death sentence.

---

52 Deuteronomy 17:2-5, "Stone that man or woman to death." The reason? Heresy.

Does it sound sensible to kill an abortionist? What about ending someone's life because you're trying to protect your personal freedom or your country's autonomy? It's no easy task to find the answers, especially when the questions about protection are honed down even further.

One example of levels of protection is if you know of a parent abusing her child. Should she be killed to stop the abuse? No, that's where we draw a line. There's hope that she can be cured of what is obviously a mental illness, or that the child can be removed from the situation. But what if you walk in and she's angrily running at the child with a knife screaming, "I'm going to kill you!" You're holding a gun, do you shoot the woman?

After all of these thought processes I return to the most commonsensical essence of ethics and morals, which is that it's rooted in your intentions. "Accidentally" having an extramarital affair could somehow happen. If you stomp out of the house after an argument with your spouse and call someone you find attractive, that's less accidental. The most obvious error is to marry someone for a reason other than love while telling yourself, "No problem, I can still go out with other people."

The larger questions, such as whether to harm or kill another person, can be put through the same processes. If the intention is ethical the act is ethical. That's my theory, in any case.

This isn't like some situations where we have ready answers, such as, "Should I report a gun owner who's threatening to kill people?" Yes. Other answers don't come readily, such as, "Should I join this war?"

When it comes to ethics, only your gut can tell you what to do. True, listening to the advice of an institution, whether it's a religion or a government, is a good start. But if a government tells you to fight a war against your personal beliefs, do you do as you're told? Saying yes is definitely an easy way out, but it might not be what's right in your gut. It would be a hard decision for someone whose religion is fully non-violent.[53]

The last thing I'll say about ethics and morals is we can think we know where we stand until we're faced with taking action. That's when we find out whether we really would kill to save another. Or on a lesser scale, whether we'd turn in an unmarked envelope filled with thousands of dollars. It is hard to pass up on free money, after all.

---

53 For example, "Ahimsa" is a non-violent aspect of religions like Buddhism and Hinduism. Gandhi used it to change his world.

Chapter 15: Money and Finances (ways of our world)

*It would be nice to spend billions
on schools and roads,
but right now that money is desperately needed
for political ads.*
— Andy Borowitz

The quote that opens this chapter references the enormous amount of ducats paid for political ads. What most people find disgusting is the amount of tax dollars elected politicians then go on to spend, and how much of that spending is for personal pleasures. Although I should qualify that sentence by noting that the most corrupt politicians are not necessarily *elected*. Sometimes they simply appear on the world stage as the result of a coup, manipulation of propaganda, or they're placed into power by a stronger but equally corrupt individual or faction.

The reason for excessive advertising is based on the glut of politicians and businesses that want all the money they can lay their hands on, for any number of personal (and occasionally altruistic) reasons. Ads are seductive because they must find a way to part us from the money we hold so dear. The attitudes of politicians, businesses, First World countries, and a majority of individuals around the planet is that more money is mo' bettah.

Nothing is taboo for those who are driven by sucking greed, no ad is too tasteless. However, most individuals just want to have some measure of financial security. We want to get by, but ideally, it's nice to be comfortable, maybe even have some fun. A vacation, a special dinner now and again, get the kids through college, these driving forces of earning an income are more sensible than the motivation of owning the world.

Worth, there's a provocative word. When it comes to our worth as individuals... let's see... "priceless" is a good way to put it because trying to place a monetary value on a human being is repugnant. I know, it's odd to say something like that in a world where "what are you worth?" is ripe with presumably positive implications. Many will disagree with my position that we cannot assume that excessive wads of cash should earn great respectability. But hey, right at the opening of this book I admitted to being a weirdo. I'm just sayin'.

I'll try to put my opinion into context with a question. Which of the following statements have the most substance?

"I'm worth a million bucks."

"You're worth everything to me."

"It's challenging to raise children, but it's worth it."

I think the theme is clear. Or here's another one: "I'd give a million bucks to wake up happy every morning." Financial worth and self-worth are like apples and aptitudes, in my mind. Both can grow if nourished, but the former is external, and the latter is internal.

How many incredible human beings from our history contributed extraordinary bounty to civilization, but died poor?

Head-counters can provide the actual number, but I'm happy knowing there was at least one Schubert, Sammy Davis Jr., Vincent van Gogh, Joe Louis, Herman Melville, Tesla, Charlie Parker, Oscar Wilde... it's a very long list. I mean, c'mon. Edgar Allan Poe, Socrates, wow. Powerful (and worthy) people, all penniless or near enough to broke when they died.

All of the names on the above list are nonconformists. It can be nice to be abnormal.

Myth of Normal

There's worth and then there's money. Money. That's another word that makes one think, perhaps with a British accent, "Quite."

Do you ever feel like you're earning enough of the stuff? Simple observations indicate that millionaires and billionaires never feel that they have enough, but that spans across all income levels. An American making $30k a year works hard and/or plays the lottery in the hope of a bigger bank account, because without it the mortgage and car payments are at risk.

How about doubling that to $60k per year? Now the house and the car are safer but medical and dental insurances are still iffy. Double it to $120k. That much income requires so much hard work that without a vacation, it's hard to keep at it. $250k a year brings a sigh of relief because now the student debt can be paid down,[54] and maybe the kids can even go to college.

Look at that, a quarter of a million dollars per year and *maybe* it's possible to catch up, with only a marginal possibility of getting ahead. Who sets these outrageous standards?

We do. We're perpetuating the myth that wealth equals happiness. This myth will stay valid as long as we believe advertising that says, "Keep up with your neighbors, toss out that faded shirt and buy another, your car works fine but it's old, replace it..." We're buying into what we're told rather than grasping the truth about happiness.

There is that age-old extreme to consider: "Would you rather die rich and alone, or poor and surrounded by loved ones?"

I'm guessing that a distressingly large number of people would pick the first option. Better lonely than poor. Surely

---

54 There's still no algorithm in my computer that will interrupt whining about academia, and the student loans that usually come with it.

they've seen movies that show the wretchedness of miserly rich guys, starting with Ebeneezer Scrooge.

Or, it could be there are too many commercials about indulging oneself, where in 2019 the Charlie and the Chocolate Factory song "I Want It Now" is used as an enticement for pleasure. Remember the moral of the song in the movie? Excessive greed is dangerous.

Today, advertising jingles about getting as much money as possible in the shortest amount of time thrive as brainworms in our heads. "Gimme gotta getme some money now all the cash now, free with no fee, just waiting for me to take it gimme gotta getme some money..."

That's pop-esque. It *reflects* culture more than it *influences* it, right? Or is it a case of the arts (including what can be astonishingly aesthetically pleasing advertising) influencing culture? Are the arts establishing our tastes and values? Hard to say, it's a chicken/egg situation, because foul artists can be rejected by consumers but sometimes the most unlikely creative endeavors start trending, even go viral. In most cases, successful artists have hit the pulse of their generation, but every now and then, an artist inspires the beat of the day.

That said, some trends never change. What I mean by that arguably oxymoronic sentence is there will always be younger generations that p'poo "old stuff," while the parents of those upstarts often cringe at "new stuff." Also, attention-getting artists and performers tap the carnal part of us, whether it's a song about sex or about a passion for acquisition in general.

Lust.

Lust is a powerful motivator, and a lusty pursuit of money (and power) is rewarded in industrialized countries. It starts while we're young and offered a few bucks to go to the movies so that parents, or siblings, can be alone. Next are prizes for competitions. Those rewards, along with the admiration, are what set us apart from the rest. We become proudly abnormal.

Despite the urge to be like everyone else, we're actively intent on becoming an outlier in the scatterplot, sliding off the bell curve toward greater and greater wealth because poverty is a dreadfully slippery skew.

Strangely, there are signs that the wealthy don't wish others to achieve this outsider status. One can't help but imagine they enjoy elitism, but that puts the kibosh on normality.

Do the super-rich *want* to be anomalies? Yes. Yes, they do. If everybody was rich first class flights would never have seats available, and there would be no way to get around crowded lines in amusement parks.

We have created a norm of seeking the highest income as possible, yet high incomes are not normal. It's no secret that very, very few people have the most amount of money in this world. It comes down to being part of the crowd by attempting to deviate from the rest. Sounds pretty goofy.

It isn't only advertising that makes us want more money and possessions. Those we admire add to our desires, whether they're rap stars and athletes weighed down by bling, or beloved talk show hosts.

Ellen DeGeneres, bless her generous heart, loves to gift people. I think Oprah can be called the first example of a talk show host giving on a large scale, and then Ellen took up the mantle (to the nth extreme). They're both so magnanimous!

However, those two women caused an evolution of thought, for me. At the time of Oprah's infamous car-giving episode I was living in Mexico, and my only income was from a tiny school I established to teach English and the martial arts to K-12 students. I had no television. It wasn't until later that my mom (Mombo) told me about the free-car episode, and her love for Oprah knew no bounds. She'd always been a fan but this put her over the top. "Oprah found an audience in need and gave each and every one of them a brand new car!"

I said, "Mombo, I wouldn't be able to receive a brand new car. There's no way I could afford the insurance or registration. Doesn't Oprah know what it's like to be poor?"

"Of course she knows!" Mombo replied, and began discussing what she had learned of the woman she so admired, but I kept thinking, "How can poor people deal with brand new cars?"

Wait—something about the above vignette kept niggling at me, and I double-checked the date that the car-giving occurred. I wasn't living in Mexico at the time, but I was in a different situation where I had no television and was extraordinarily low-income (again). Maybe the way to gain a true understanding poverty is related to its frequency in one's life?

Back to the point: Ellen becomes the next angel of the airwaves, giving away massive amounts of cash to her audience, and also many, many products. Over the years I continued thinking, "I wouldn't be able to receive those physical gifts. There's no room in my wee home."

The gifted products seem extravagant and unnecessary for people who have trouble paying monthly bills. The deeper irony is people have tried to sell the gifts but were shamed by Ellen, on camera, in later episodes.

It got even stranger when during a 2019 episode,[55] a guest named Alyson Stoner told Ellen she had given away all her possessions. She had many heartfelt reasons for taking that

---

[55] September 9.

Myth of Normal

step, including feeling put off by wild luxury. Alyson said the decision to let go of so many things had given her a feeling of weightlessness.

Ellen responded by giving Alyson a 65" TV. Alyson received it graciously, but she noted, "It won't even fit in my studio."

Things that make ya go "Huh?"

Some recipients of Ellen's gifts live in a studio apartment because that's all they can afford.

Returning to the point, it has crossed my mind that the longer someone sustains wealth, the weaker the grasp on the realities of low-income and poverty living. Then I thought about all the other philanthropic endeavors of O and E. Gifting products and possessions is only a facet of their giving; they have other profound depths of generosity. They dig deep for scholarships and charities, they support causes that save women and children, and yup, they help regular fellas, too.

The question does remain, why give a 65" TV to someone who clearly expressed a desire to *not* have a possession like that? Those TVs are expensive. I also don't get why she'd give one to any person whose needs are much larger – like a job, or a living space that can fit a giant TV.

Acquisition is a leading aspect of American norms. As it turns out, both Ellen and Oprah have dealt with living the low-income life, and in the U.S., striving for a high income in order to surround oneself with goodies is a standard. It's a motivator. Sadly, it can also be an embarrassment for those who are poor.

Just a sec, here are some kickers: a DeGeneres-fan friend told me Ellen *has* employed some viewers, or helped people find jobs. Apparently she has also done some home makeovers for fans, even helping them to get homes, and now she has an even bigger giveaway show. Also, she has given away a half-million dollars. The recipients are a family to whom she recently gave all 12 days of her program's Christmas gifts. Now they can buy a house to fit the gifts! It gets better, too, because she and her Cheerios™ sponsor gave them an additional half-million so that they can pay it forward.

We humans, we can be so complex. That million dollar giveaway was something. It goes beyond giving low-income people a gift they can't afford to own, it recognizes that the poor are different. The idea of including a way to help others, that's brilliant.

A friend who once worked for tips told me, "I was always relieved when I saw someone driving an inexpensive car, wearing mid-range clothing, because I knew I'd get a better tip. It was the rich people who'd give a few coins or a buck, but the un-rich were giving three, or a fiver."

In that friend's experience, the more money someone had the less they gave away. I guess that's why they have so much; they cling to what they have.

Pure selfish greed is sad, I can't help but think there are those who sincerely wish they could take their money with them when they died, if it were possible. It makes me wonder about such a person's faith in what comes after life on Earth. More of the same? Class systems, rich and poor, acquisition—which these days are products *designed* to break so that the manufacture can make more money...[56] Ugh.

I should put all this into the context of a relatively new sub-discipline of psychology called "positive psychology," where the focus is on what works for us rather than what's wrong with us. In the early stages of that sub-discipline, studies were conducted that measured the theory of happiness relating to income. For many, it seemed a given that wealth can be

---

56 Planned obsolescence.

used to purchase glorious contentment, and so experts decided to test that notion.

In the theory of better income equaling greater happiness, positive psychologists ask big questions, like whether wealth increases one's chance of receiving loving devotion. Or, can high-buckage help you feel assured of—and able to sustain—physical health? Can money enable one to be assured of—and able to sustain—mental peace?

Can money buy freedom?

Surely there's ample evidence of the connection between coinage and contentment. Would that the experts agreed.

Psychologists in general disagree, but with each other. Well-paid researchers are paid well because they're talented, and also because they're accomplished at finding correlations between the pursuit of money and happiness. When they're paid well they experience the very phenomenon they're studying. On the other hand, lowlier soldiers of science may be jaded by their low-income status, meaning there are conflicts of interest on both sides. Will we ever know the truth?

If I had money to throw around I'd bet a lot that well-funded researchers are happy with saying, "It couldn't be more obvious that financial superiority creates superior satisfaction." It isn't cheap to prove a hypothesis, which is why some regular researchers will say what funders want to hear.

Positive psychologists, on the other hand, often come from a place of poverty – again, it's hard to get funding for new or unpopular ideas. Misfit studies declare novel findings, which are priceless, and many positive psychologists assert that money is not a reliable source of happiness.

All that said, it's understandable that we hope there's a significant correlation between wealth and satisfaction. There are examples of love for sale, seeing as how obnoxious, unattractive wealthy men can seduce affectionate women of mesmerizing beauty.[57] In our world it takes money, and lots of it, to survive poor health. The cost of a house, a car, utilities, food, and keeping ones' teeth functioning without pain, it's all as jarring as a kick in the... anyway.

I find it repugnant that cures exists for all manner of physical ailments, but those who cannot afford them cannot, and will not, be cured. I personally know someone who almost died from sepsis because she couldn't come up with the capital for dental care! Her doctor had to stomp down to the authorization department and say, "I'm telling you that without proper dental care, my patient will die. It needs to be included in her physical health care plan. Now."

It's no exaggeration to say that poverty can kill a person, and so the Vulcan logic "live long" includes "prosper," dictating that wealth is directly proportionate to long life.

Those with the most bucks can buy love and physical health, and I suppose mental health is buyable, too. An example of the last is seeing police lights flashing in your rear-view mirror after you've shared a bottle of wine at dinner. It's enough to cause a nervous breakdown over the progression of possibilities; will you lose your job, your license? How much is this going to cost? Your spouse might leave you. *You will go to jail.*

If you're rich enough, those concerns can be flicked aside. You won't lose your job because you run the place,[58] and you don't care so much about your license because you could hire a driver for a while. No worries about financial repercussions, and the spouse isn't going anywhere without

---

57 Juries deliberate on whether women marrying for money have icky scruples.
58 Or you were born with silk stockings

access to your yacht and private jet.

If you've got enough bounty in the bank, *you will not go to jail.*

After all of those pro-wealth arguments, it's still my personal opinion that money is not a strict requirement of life satisfaction, nor does acquisition ensure happiness. It would take millennia to prove this statement, but I'll say it anyway: a foundation of joy and appreciation for the smaller elements of living can bring happiness whether one is bucks-up or down.

I've talked about the subjectivity of well-being, and there really is a lot of meat in that mindset. If you're contented despite a low pay-grade you've got it made. Many have experienced euphoria that has nothing to do with their wallets, and hopefully you are one of those people. That's all the evidence one needs to answer the question of where joy can be found.

Price is objective. It's incidental to what's best for our lives.

Just like pain, joy is everywhere. It's the way of the world, that we will sometimes be exultant and at other times we'll scrape the bottom of a misery chasm. It's a flip of an existential coin, day after day. Despite all that, many of us wish that coin were made of gold.

Wait – what happens when a coin lands on its edge? Is that an indicator of tedium, with no highs or lows in income or happiness?

A coin landing on edge could be explained as coincidence, or magic, or simple science. Or, if you're superstitious, you might think it has something to do with luck.

R.L. George

Chapter 16: Supernatural Superstitions

> *Men are probably nearer
> the essential truth
> in their superstitions
> than in their science.*
> –Thoreau

The word "supernatural" pretty much breaks down to that which is outside the realm of reality. Extra-normal. "Superstition" isn't as clear cut as that—it's more personal—but the implication is what we believe to be supernatural is what sets us apart. Reality and superstition are seen as opposites, because in theory most people don't honestly believe stepping on cracks or walking under a ladder will change anybody's luck.

I'd guess most of us have some manner of superstitious behaviors, even if we're not aware of what causes a knock on wood or a "bless you" when someone sneezes. I don't know if those idiosyncrasies are any more rational than chanting anti-voodoo spells, buying potions for love, or making New Year's resolutions.

Evidently voodoo works, but only on those who truly believe it will. It does not work on those who truly believe it won't. There's bound to be a psychological explanation for that, but that won't erase its real impact the believers.

As far as I've heard, New Year's resolutions don't work, although they seem more reasonable. Fresh year, fresh start and all that.

An ancient ancestor looking at our world today would see magic, so of course we can push that forward to how the future would look to us. The point is knowledge and science would eventually be able to explain everything that appears to be magical or miraculous, but I'm not buying it. One element of magic is surprise, that not knowing. For example, not knowing what happens after we die is arguably the most enduringly enigmatic aspect of life.

When it comes to how certain phenomena really happen, science is bound to offer answers someday. Yet I honestly don't care *how* I experienced a magical moment, I only care that I did.

Our beliefs are bound up in the traditions we learned in church, in the town or city around us, or on grandparents' knees. It's likely we're doing pack-like thinking more often than we're setting off into our own minds. There are extremes that wander into OCD-land, where every fencepost must be tapped and all foods in the kitchen must be alphabetically arranged. What I prefer to talk about here is the middle-ground, the center, rather than those who live in the outer edges.

That outer space (so to speak) is nearer to each of us than we'd like to think. Instinctive reactions to the world around us are as close as a salt shaker accidentally thrown over your shoulder, even if you think you don't give a toss about old wives' tales.

Friday the 13th is a good example, because it's an oddly rational reaction to feel cursed if, say, you were once fired from a job on that day. The memory will come back because the day is notable, and you'll be on your guard. There's tension in that that *en garde* posture throughout that day, and like stress, too much tension can cause mistakes with alarming consequences. It would be easy to continue associating bad luck with Friday the 13th.

We do it all the time, where we associate a mind-and-body-memory of pain or anguish with a significant date.[59] It's obvious that people will remember details of intense physical injury and any event that's horrific or exalted. They also know where they were and exactly what they were doing when a huge storm or earthquake happened in the place where they live.

There's science behind all that, such as adrenaline enhancing memory, but it took a while for us to figure that out. It wasn't enough to accept that special memories happen, we had to know why.

Scientists sure do love their evidence, so much so that in the past they've been unwilling to accept anything outside their own realm of facts. "Round Earth? Great flood? Black holes? Prove it." Somebody proves it, controversies ensue, and scientists resist for as long as they can. At last, they begrudgingly admit, "I might have been wrong," and *kapow*! We have a new fact.

Many are convinced a thing is only real if it's provable. That's very strange in light of the difficulties in "proving" something like love, which is the most astounding experience of life—outside of life itself, of course.[60]

It can be argued that a mother's love is measurable in scientific tests that point to biological reactions. Chemical and magnetic ingredients are in play when two adults fall in love. However, that type of evidence may prove that love exists, but not *why*.

Further still, we don't know how these fluctuations

---

[59] They referred to that once on an old episode of M*A*S*H* (I say that like there are new episodes). In "Death Takes a Holiday" (1980), the doctors try to keep a soldier alive long enough to say that he died *after* Christmas day, all for the sake of ensuring the family memories of the holiday aren't saturated with sadness.

[60] As of the time of this writing, there are still no universally accepted theories of how life came to be.

manifest as the phenomenon we identify as "love." Science will attempt to answer those questions sooner or later. "Humanity factor One causes a reaction of chemical factor Two which fires various synapses" and so on, ad nauseam. Voila! The dual mysteries of how and why love occurs are solved.

Deeper into the quagmire of the scientific need for proof is that the "humanity factor" must be flung into the equation, yet that factor still needs more details. Love may be an important facet of human beings continuing as a race, but where did we come from, how did we get here, and (I saved the big one for last) why is there such a thing as a human race?

It crosses my mind that a race who discovers or provides the answers to those last questions would be more than human. Say, supernatural, or extra-normal. Superhuman, or godlike. If some outside entity doesn't clue us in, it'll be up to us humans to figure it out. We're always gathering more information, and surely someday we'll find what we're looking for.

Is that what we really want?

I think a driving desire to ascend to godlike status does exist in the human psyche, or in the viscera. I'm amazed by how many people wish they could live forever, which is to say, they want to be immortal. Silly thing is, we have no evidence that we *aren't* immortal, as in continuing to exist in some other fashion after we've finished being human. Does science hope to prove that to be true? Scientists could just as easily ascertain that we're gone after we die, that we simply end forever. Who would want to know that?

Myth, tradition, and religions offer hope of an afterlife, even if they do suggest some dour turns if one is not following certain tenets. Regulations and morals of stories abound, but while the laws are meant to help us live well, mythical morals often guide us toward doing well after death.

The possibility of a crummy afterlife is scary. The leaders of nations, powers that be, and regulators are afraid of myth, I think. I've heard that Washington D.C. was laid out with a mathematical precision because the founding fathers wanted to focus on reason rather than religion. That notion wasn't in response to Christianity or Judaism, Paganism or Buddhism. All spiritual ideologies were meant to be shut out of a country's governance, which means we're back to facts while ignoring concepts like love and God or gods, respect for animals and nature, exploration of inner spaces, and superstitions.

Leaders who try to set aside those aspects of humanity hope to expand their realm of governance to include all diverse people. That doesn't mean our quirks around superstitions aren't charming. And religions are often a source of comfort and hope. Myth, legends, and belief in the supernatural have a crucial place in every culture, and we're better off if we honor that fact rather than try to brush it away.

We may not share the same folklore, but we're all sharing this globe. Love and sociability and friendship, these are driving forces of living a good life. Let's give ourselves props for being silly, complicated, wonderful human beings surrounded by more of the same.

Chapter 17: Connections

> *Friendship is born at that moment*
> *when one person says to another:*
> *'What! You too? I thought I was the only one.'*
> — C.S. Lewis

Everyone knows that yelling at someone will get a reaction. They'll holler back at you, or be cowed, or they'll turn and walk away. Maybe the person will laugh. The fact remains that some response will occur, and the same is true if we kiss someone, or strike another person. However, it can be hard to believe that our thoughts and behaviors affect people we've never met, those who are outside our immediate sphere.

I'm convinced that it can happen. What we think and do reverberates around the globe. The effect of a single wee butterfly is one thing, purported to have enough power to cause storms on the other side of the planet. Human capacity is something else altogether.

Thinkers like C.G. Jung have talked about a collective consciousness. Scientists like physicist rock star Fontini Markopoulou have discussed the interconnectivity of humans between one another, and with the world around them. Einstein, too, he had that "entanglement" theory of particle physics, which is named well enough to figure out its point.

Native Americans are credited with recognizing the connections between everything, all of it, and in a number of religions, there's a "oneness" for individuals to strive toward.[61] I'm a fan of all styles of thought, but the way we humans and

---

61 Hinduism is an example.

the universe around us are all connected, wow. Those types of mental puzzles are so distracting that I avoid starting on them while driving or reading a book. I won't go deep thinking about it while standing in the shower, because I might run out of hot water before I've finished washing.

There's a Global Consciousness Project that can be found online, and it is awe inspiring. It electronically measures human reactions around the world when there are major events, like earthquakes and the 911 attacks. Collectively, our reactions as a global society are *scientifically measurable*. Oh. em. gee.

All of this sounds difficult to swallow, but if it can be accepted as true it would have a remarkable impact. I'll talk more about that in a moment, but first, how can it be believed? If you're skeptical as you're reading this, how can I convince you?

A word: "Stransers."

The way that word came about was through conversations with friends about an odd but common phenomenon. It starts when you're watching TV or walking down the street, reading a book or listening to the radio. You'll think of something you hadn't thought of for years, like, "Where's Waldo?," or something obscure, like "I wonder how many people have heard of ollalieberries?" Or, you'll think about how you used to love cherry pie, but you haven't had any for decades.

Then, a TV show comes on and a character says, "I thought of going as Waldo this Halloween, but I worried that none of my friends would be able to find me." Later you're reading a book and the author says, "I like ollalieberry muffins but I prefer cherry pie."

I've talked with quite a few people about this over many years, and most have had similar experiences. Only a few have no idea what I'm talking about, but once the phenomenon gets into their heads, they start noticing it, too.

It's a strange serendipity to think of something unusual and then have it show up from somewhere outside of you. *Strange serendipity* is how my friends and I came up with the word "stranser." The experience is curiouser still when there's a run of them, an example being something that happened with my Mombo.

I chose "cherry pie" above because that was the source of one of Mombo's stransers. One day she remembered how she used to love those pies, it was just a passing thought. The next day her son-in-law walked in and held out a cherry pie, announcing, "Look what I got for dessert!" She hadn't made a peep to him about her own thought.

The day after that she got a newspaper and saw a recipe with the title, "What Ever Happened to Cherry Pie?" The day after that, she stumbled across an old TV show where her idol, George Carlin, played the doo-wop song, "Cherry Pie."[62] Mombo was such a fan of Carlin, and she hadn't even known he could play piano!

She had a triple-stranser, and I have had the same experience, and friends have had it happen too. It wouldn't surprise me if I were to lie down tonight with a fiction novel and see a cherry pie reference. And that is part of my fascination with stransers; if you pay attention, you can start finding them everywhere.

Over the years, my friends and I accepted the reality of stransers being a thing, but we had a little more trouble trying to figure out what they *meant*. They don't feel like ESP, so how do they happen? It was Mombo who finally discovered the forest through the trees: they're about interconnectivity.

---

62 Originally by Marvin & Johnny, 1954

R.L. George

When you're walking through life and you experience something beyond coincidence, it has that supernatural feel. I'm arguing that it isn't *super*natural, it's *extra*-natural. It's outside our usual understanding of the world, but it's natural and extraordinarily important. Stransers could somehow show us the best paths while we muddle through our day-to-day.

I'm hoping you've had stransers, now that they have a name, because if you have, it means you can see them as evidence for connectivity with everyone and everything in this world.

Although Mombo came up with my favorite answer about what stransers mean, I still didn't understand *why* they happen. It wasn't until after she died that it hit me: they serve as indicators of how connected one is with the world and its people. For better or worse.

That realization came at a time that I noticed more stransers than usual—they seem to come in waves, then they back off for a while—and when I found that I was experiencing a plethora of stransers, I also realized my life wasn't as rocky as life can often be. Back when that happened I thought something to the effect of, "Wouldn't it be nice if one could actively seek out stransers, and they would somehow make life a little more bearable?"

Soon after that I began going through some more rough patches, as we all do, and once I came up for air long enough to think about something other than my challenges, it occurred to me that I hadn't noticed any stransers lately. That was when I began actively seeking them out, and sure enough, when I saw more of them my life got better. Not in some vague, possibly coincidental way, but noticeably so. In some cases there were inexplicable, unexpected improvements.

Who knows what's going on behind all this, but I want to continue keeping my mind open to, or for, stransers.

Myth of Normal

They've happened while I've been writing this very book. I always have music or TV on in the background for white noise, and as I was adding a Will Rogers quote some snippet about Rogers will arise from the outside world. Or, I'll be writing about hippie beads and while I'm in the grocery store that afternoon, I'll overhear someone say, "My daughter was born in the 1990s but she dresses like a hippie, beads and all."

Maybe, just maybe, stransers not only show how we're connected with life, they can also cause it.

What I'm thinking is they're always out there, kind of like miracles that no one notices but they're happening all the time anyway. In the case of stransers, seeking them out and taking notice of them can help us subconsciously choose the best path.

By "path" I don't necessarily mean which career goal is best, although that would be included. But I also refer to small decisions, like whether or not to have salad with dinner – you decide not to, and then discover the lettuce you were going to use has been recalled due to e-coli concerns.

I guess what I'm saying is all the information is out there, and it's a matter of capturing what we need. Stransers may be one way of tapping in. Who knows why, and as I said earlier about magic, I'm not sure I need the science to tell me what's going on. I want to expand my awareness however I can, even if it seems superstitious. Some superstitions are grounded in fact, after all.[63]

Many pages have been spent here on stransers and interconnectivity, although this is a book about what's normal (or not). The reason I've given focus to this topic is because life without others would be unbearable, and relationships are

---

63 I remember once reading about superstitious hand-washing to wash away bad luck, and catching something like e-coli sounds pretty unlucky to me.

built on interconnections. At times, connecting with others is the result of some strange serendipity.

Those who feel very lonely, and worry about being too weird, need to know that although they're special, they're not abnormal. I suspect loneliness is related to being off a step from connecting, and I think it can be remedied by seeking out stransers. Nothing to lose, everything to gain.

Many of us spend quite a bit of time seeing ourselves as being a bit off. So much time that we end up missing the fact that everyone else is feeling the same way. We are all flawed, some just hide it better than others. Flaws and qualities exist in those we idolize or genuinely love, and we can address that fact in a healthy fashion.

I'm a very loving person, but it didn't take long to realize that I can love some people and still not like them. If someone I love is toxic to my life, I won't spend time with that individual. I love him or her, but I don't interact. That's fine.

However, if we become aware that a loved one's flaws are outweighed by wonderful qualities, we should interact with that person. When we do interact we ought to let go of all frustration about the flaws, and accept that person as-is. In other words, if we know their faults aren't hurting us, don't sweat the small stuff. Concentrate on the great gift that is love, family, and/or friendship.

(Later) I finished writing the above paragraph and then took a break to stretch out with a good old-fashioned newspaper. Before long I was reading about how my newspaper is adjusting their restaurant star-rating system, based on a few reasons. One of the reasons is related to a restaurant's quality: "Is it so compelling that you won't mind its flaws?"[64]

---

64 Staff Reports, Arizona Republic, July 10 2019

Myth of Normal

I read that within thirty minutes of writing about my stranser concept. That's another thing about stransers – they take different forms. This time it wasn't about a word or thing, it was about the idea of acceptance despite flaws, and to hear it echoed so closely, so quickly, is exhilarating. All that is aside from the fact that not long before, I wrote about how a stranser would probably leap out at me specifically because I was writing about them.

The connected world is all a part of nature, and like nature, it can awe us with its beauty and power.

Now I'll return to my comments about acceptance. I've said this before and here it comes again, as it will again in the future: acceptance is indescribably helpful in living a happier life. When you choose to interact with those you love, please accept them as they are, flaws and all. Interactions will be so much more pleasant. If their flaws are too much, accept *that* as the way things are, and although you're not able to hang out together, you still get to love the person.

That approach makes life easier. Conflict is inherently unpleasant, whether it's external or internal. And speaking of internal conflict, I think one of the most amazing things a person can do is to accept his or her self. When you're okay with who you are it's easier for others to be okay with who you are.

I understand that self-acceptance isn't easy, otherwise it would be commonplace. Part of the difficulty lies in truly knowing oneself. This is hard to hear, but sometimes what we dislike in others is a fault we find in ourselves. That can be intimidating to think about, because there are people you don't like based on their bad attitude, or they're too cranky or unpleasant.

Does all of that sound unbelievable? Whether or not one believes in something doesn't mean it doesn't exist, pardon the double-negative. It's like saying, "I don't believe in setting a minimum wage," but minimum wages have been set. They do exist.

Who you are is a finely woven, artistic quilt, and although some of the squares are quite appealing, others require a discerning eye to find the beauty in them. I'll try to explain all of this as best as I can...

Chapter 18: The Scintillating Self

> *Many people are
> normally this crazy.*
> – R.L. George

I remember sitting in the passenger seat while a friend was driving, her eyes on the rear-view mirror, grumbling about the tailgating car behind us. I was looking ahead, and we were only a few feet from the bumper of the car in front of us.

Throughout my life, I've learned that nobody benefits from the presence of a nervous passenger. Quietly, secretly pressing a non-existent brake pedal will relieve some stress, but screeching "Look out!" can cause an accident as much as prevent one. It's hard to say whether any reaction will be useful, though. The calmest suggestion to reduce speed during a gusting hailstorm can be met with contempt by an arrogant driver.

At the time my friend complained about tailgating while doing so herself, I pointed forward and asked (in a voice that sounded curious, not accusatory), "So this is the best distance?"

My friend focused in front of her and was thoughtful for a moment. Our distance behind the front car gradually increased. At last my friend admitted, "I didn't realize I was doing that. Usually, I don't. I'm actually a very good driver. I was distracted by the idiot behind us and it made me do the same stupid thing."

Don't protest too much, now.

I'm reminded of those who really are capable drivers, but they abuse their talents by zipping through traffic like trained racers. The problem is that the other people on the road are not trained as racers, and they're intimidated when the speedy driver weaves past, missing bumpers by millimeters. After speedy is gone, singing, "I'm such a good driver," accidents happen in his wake.

When we have a talent it's hard to acknowledge our faulty facets. A man who has dated numerous beautiful women may think about how people tend to be drawn toward others of a similar appearance. However, he may not be conventionally attractive; he's just charismatic (or rich). It might not sit well with him to learn that he's not a movie-star lookalike.

Under the skin we might think we're good drivers,[65] or excellent cooks, or calm in an emergency, etc., but we may not be so. It can be sad to learn otherwise, and downright scary if it's a more intimidating type of self-belief that's not true. The best example is to be diagnosed with some kind of mental illness, but I'll talk about milder possibilities.

It could be that you talk too much (who, me?) when in fact you always thought you were a good listener (I believe some people can do both). Another possibility is that you assumed you were right about something for many years, but it turns out you're wrong. In other words, some undeniably convincing evidence comes to light and you realize you've been wrong for ages.

It's unsettling to be wrong, and harder still to judge others about something we suspect is true of ourselves, even if our suspicions are subconscious. "He talks too much, she's not a great cook." The intensity of dislike for the flaws of another could be directly proportional to concerns about one's

---

[65] Odds are you do think you're a better driver than most, it's a thing for people to think that of themselves.

own failings in those areas.

Many Germans in the 1930s and 40s said, "Only fools don't support Hitler." No foolin', back in the day there were countless everyday Germans who said that. How horrifyingly wrong can a citizen be to support politicians like Hitler, Idi Amin, or Robert Mugabe? There is a fairly rational excuse for such massively mistaken opinions. Wrong decisions are sparked by propaganda, simple as that. It's kind of like brainwashing but it's more like brain-dirtying. When it comes to getting what one wants out of masses of people, propaganda is a heady force.

I remember when I was younger, the news was provided as information, not opinion. I'm pretty sure that remains true of local news broadcasts. Otherwise, I've noticed people tend to pick one cable news source or another, but rarely watch both sides. I recommend watching neutral news or both types of cable sources, because it's best to avoid being lopsided. That way if something leaps out to show that you've been wrong about what you believed from the news, you're not off-balance, and won't be as easily knocked over.

Seriously, I cannot imagine what it must have been like for some good people who supported Mugabe, and found many reasons to praise him until his dictator-attitude became undeniable. Who knows, maybe there *are* those who feel safer under a dictatorship. Personally, it would make me feel like a piece of wet cardboard. Useless as an individual, with no place in the backbone of my very own country. Those who live in dictatorships have no voice.

Voices take on different tones, for instance whether one is voting, blogging, or sitting on a jury. The last can serve as an illustration of learning, embarrassingly, that one was not in possession of enough information to have a proper understanding of the situation. To be sequestered while on a jury means it's a famous trial, but the jurors miss out on some significant facts. Defense attorneys manipulate legal minutia to keep details out of the trial.

During the OJ Simpson trial in the 1990s, the jury was sequestered and didn't have access to the news—and evidence—seen by the public. I've heard of at least one juror who was startled to learn about what was held back from the courtroom, and said the verdict might have been different if all the evidence had been available to the jury.

Admitting one is wrong is courageous. If one is wrong and won't accept it, the reaction often manifests as anger, hatred, even violence. That's immature, and I can admit that because there have been times when was pretty mad about being wrong. Never violent about it, but I'm ashamed to say, childish.

I'd like to point out the difference between being childish and being childlike. A childlike adult will joyfully jump on the thin film of ice over a puddle in the winter. A childish adult who's watching will grimace and say, "Don't be such a child."

I hope to hold onto my own youthful joy long after I'm dead.

Returning to general assumptions about the self and others, *pre*sumptions happen, too. An example is when it comes to what I call, "states of sheveled." Like everything else, our personal grooming is a matter of perspective. Some women wear makeup and others don't, a man with a perfect, precise haircut wears wrinkled clothing, a little girl who insists on carrying a pretty handkerchief never uses it to wipe her nose. It's hard to tell what people are thinking.

I once met an otherwise nappy man whose eyeglasses were so dirty it made me want to ask him if he had any eyedrops. Instead I asked, "Can I see your glasses?" He said,

Myth of Normal

"I assume so, but I can't." I had just met the guy, but I was pulling out a tissue to use as a wipe. "Let me clean them for you," I offered.

"I'll get to it later."

"I don't mind, let me have them."

"No."

We went our separate ways, and at the time I thought he was an odd dude. Here was a person who went out of his way to go to an eye-doctor, correct his vision with framed pieces of glass (or plastic), and yet he was blinded by what, laziness? Optical apathy?

In retrospect I wonder what he was hiding. Eyes, windows, soul, all that, he may have been afraid of exposing himself. It wasn't until years later that it occurred to me, if a stranger asked to see my glasses, would I hand them over? I meet someone at a party, he or she is carrying the scent of Zinfandel and a tissue and is forcefully requesting my glasses. Kooky.

Yet upon further reflection, yes, I would let somebody clean my glasses. It isn't like prescription lenses would be worth stealing. A stranger offering to pluck my eyebrows, that would be different.

There are bound to be people out there who wish they could change something about their appearance, yes, including something as benign as eyebrows. I've seen actors from the olden days with eyebrows that could be combed back to hide a bald spot. Whoopi Goldberg has no eyebrows at all. There's no real standard, so when a stranger or even a friend wants to change us, it's not a bad idea to question their motives. We're fine as we are, that's my story and although I might do some editing, I won't change the theme.

This doesn't mean we can't be grateful that others care enough to offer a lens wipe, or that we have eyes at all.

R.L. George

Gratitude, I've noticed it has become a thing, to consciously note those things for which we are grateful. I've heard about thanks for family, work, good weather, touchdowns, home runs, and so on, but I think we must also be grateful to the self.

As an example, say you made yourself stop to get gas even though you were very tired. Next thing you know, there's a citywide blackout! Now you have a full tank and everyone else is scrambling for fuel. Thank yourself for taking care of business even when you didn't feel like it.

Once you get into gratitude it's easier to keep track of minor miracles. I've had times when I felt intense gratitude solely because a whole day passed without some drastic turn or irritating difficulty.

I recently had a few hard days, where I started the morning with a terrible toothache, my car broke down the next day, and the day after that my hot water heater sprung a leak, soaking the bathroom, sagging the floors. These things really did happen. Ugh, what a pileup.

Then I dropped a favorite glass, and it somehow didn't break. It remains unbroken to this day![66] I was so grateful! And what a relief when a big branch fell during a storm and nothing at all was damaged. I guess the roughest times can be offset by gratitude for the smaller crashes that *don't* happen.

My bottom line is to be happy about having the things that you do cherish. Context helps, like comparing the stress of a leaky roof with no roof over your head at all.

The same can be said for any issues a person has with personal appearance. If you have a pot belly or a double chin, own it. Embrace it. Next time you see a friend or beloved family member whose looks you like, remember that they're

---

[66] Knock wood. I take superstition with a grain of sea salt, but I'm not taking any chances.

Myth of Normal

seeing their own flaws, while all you're seeing is this loving person. You're seeing the whole individual rather than picking apart faults. That's respect, to admire the entirety of the loved one while disregarding any real or perceived drawbacks.

I recommend showing yourself the same respect as you show others.

Your authentic self is worthy of you. No one else is a perfect, or better, you. You are the original, the template. If you think you're freakish, go with it. And remember that the word was given a positive slant, back in the day, thanks to the song Superfreak.[67]

---

[67] Rick James. 1981. This song drifted out of the cray-cray decades of the 1960s and 70s.

R.L. George

Chapter 19: Conformity

He that respects himself is safe from others.
He wears a coat of mail that none can pierce.
— Longfellow

I've studied conformity academically, and it's pretty grim. There are articles about the dangers of conforming to authoritarian tenets like, "Spare the rod, spoil the child," because that child might grow up to abuse his own. Or, there are women who believe they have no choice but to conform to allowing themselves to be objectified. Children go along with crowds into drug and alcohol abuse. Entire nations decide to kill off a faction or race of people because hey, that's the done thing. Just following the mob.

Are there any positive studies about joining the lemmings in a suicidal plunge? (Positive studies about that? It's oxymoronic.) (I know, I'm wearing my opinions about conformity on my sleeve.) The answer is no, there are no positive studies on the subject, not that I've found. The closest excuse for being part of the pack is with regard to avoiding rejection, because rejection is painful, so go ahead and beat on your kids. Or wear sexy high-heeled shoes that deform the feet and wreck the back because that's what it takes to keep up with the fashion times. Or the Joneses. Whatever.

I don't need to admit that the idea of conformity gives me the creeps, because it's written all over this book.

Here's a way to look at it: going along with others for no reason other than to avoid rejection means you are giving up your own mind. Does your opinion matter to you? How could you let other people form your ideas for you? Even as a child, I was mortified by ideas that were sold to me as education. They presented ephemeral ideas as facts, and brooked no questions about the validity because there it was, in black and white, in the textbook.

I distinctly remember saying to a teacher, in grade school, "Manifest Destiny sounds like an excuse." The teacher waved me off. "But," I persisted, "anyone who takes over any other country could just use the same excuse. Would you want another country to take us over and say the same thing?"

Because I have no memory of a response, I'm guessing nothing rational or articulate was offered.

I have had good teachers, but some would receive an "F" grade from mini-me.[68] Maybe would should morph teaching into a top-paying job to ensure we'll get top-notch educators talking to our kids.

It can drive adults to distraction to hear a child ask "why" a thousand times. There's some thirsty knowledge going on in those forming brains, and they're asking "why" as much to hear a pat answer as it is to understand the machinations of their own minds.

That's confusing, I'll try to clear it up with the classic "blue sky" questioning session. Say a child looks up and thinks, "The sky is blue because it's my favorite color," and then asks a parent in order to confirm that theory. A smart parent gives the real answer, it has to do with scattered sunlight particles n'such. Do they think that's all the kid wanted to know? "Whatcha talking about, Mom?" Who *wouldn't* want to know why sunlight particles scatter?

The child formulates another theory, visualizing possibilities based on what little information they've had time

---

68 And, I confess, major me with all my degrees. But some algorithm in my computer is cutting off my whine—

to gather in their short span of life. Light. Scattering. Colors. "Why does that happen?" comes the inevitable question.

A tired parent would respond, "Manifest destiny." A cruel parent would reply, "Because I said so." (The reason I think that's cruel is because the child is being taught that one must believe, without further questions, everything one hears, reads, and sees in places like TV and Facebook.)

Despite the standard examples of conformative thinking that we're battered with throughout childhood, adults somehow learn to think for themselves. In fact, doing your own thinking is the common expectation (ask anyone who's been charged with accessory to a crime). That's why it's confusing that others try very hard, quite often, to do our thinking for us.

I've heard that after a catastrophe people look to their leaders to help them understand what happened. I can see why; if a major storm hits everyone wants to know from government leaders how and where to find help, and if lives are lost people turn to religious leaders to help with emotional pain management.

Government leaders will direct us when we make an error that will hurt others, and religious leaders guide us if we have a lapse of judgment that will hurt our own lives. In what situations do we learn our own lessons, make our own judgment calls?

The ready answer is tied to the goals we set for ourselves. Humans strive for many things, but there are some basics. Some measure of security, yes, but what is it about feeling secure in your ability to have food and shelter that's so important? Survival *and* happiness. Yet as important as feelings of security, happiness and comfort are, conformity is evidently more magnetic.

A nice car is a lovely possession, but it can't be the only reason to smile. Important goals aren't purchased, they're

Myth of Normal

achieved. We know these things intuitively, but find ourselves pursuing a nice car to the neglect of other options, like spending time with the children. The nicer the car, the more hours must be spent working, or at least that's what we've been told. Work hard so you can gain plenty... money. Possessions.

It really is a good feeling to have a pretty car that can be trusted to work well. It's also nice to have more than a tar & gravel roof over a walk-up studio apartment. The conformity problem arises when we must have that newer vehicle, no matter that the old one looks and works fine. Or a new phone that costs more than the very first car you owned,[69] despite the fact that the current cell has all the bells, whistles, and cameras you'll ever need.

Possessions are fun but they're distractions from goals like maintaining physical and mental health. It's no little irony that a physically and mentally healthy person has less trouble buying fun possessions. There wouldn't be a stigma about being "crazy" if the crazy ones were the most successful.

---

[69] I've seen cellphone prices as high as $2,500 for a single unit! My first car cost $600, admittedly less of a bargain when I remember that in order to reverse, I had to open my door and push with my left leg.

R.L. George

Chapter 20: Compos Mentis?

*I became insane,
with long intervals of horrible sanity.*
– Edgar Allan Poe

Mental health. That term carries an underlying cringe, which is too bad, because health is ya know, good for ya.

I think there are a few reasons for discomfort with the term "mental health." For one thing, its opposite is immediately brought to mind, and it feels worse than the opposite of physical health.

If you're not healthy the first thing someone might think is, "Do you have a cold?" When mental health is specified, as in, "I'm not mentally healthy," what's the first thing that comes to mind?

Looney. Nuts. Possibly even coconuts.

Despite all that nervousness about the topic, mental health is in an ongoing state of flux. This is true for every human being. Those who say "It's not true for me!" have never had a child, or a breakup, or a bi-polar episode like winning $10,000 in a casino and then having their car's transmission drop to the asphalt the next day.

Whether or not a person is diagnosable as mentally ill is outside the scope of this book. What I prefer to emphasize is whether or not *you* think you're crazy when really, you're not. If the majority of the human population were insane, it would be so obvious that we wouldn't all walk around questioning our sanity as often as we do.

Emotions ride on a tilt-a-whirl of internal and external forces. On a broader scale, there's a part of me that thinks

Myth of Normal

every four to eight years, one half of the politically-minded people in the United States are clinically depressed. Individual challenges, on the other hand, range from dealing with spooky aches and pains to work pressures to enduring the stress of family problems.

When it comes to the mind of our private selves, it's hard to judge the soundness of our own thoughts. You can worry less, though, if you remember that old adage about how people who really are insane never question their sanity.

People tend to think that others think the way they do, but that's rarely what's going on. That's why it can be stunning to find out someone really did give you a gift without expecting anything in return, while you're one who always expects something back when you give. Conversely, it can be startling to learn that a man shot his wife, they were your neighbors, all seemed "normal," you had no idea it would happen. The reason is because it would never cross your mind to shoot anybody.

The way others see us is a different story. Depending on who you're talking to, you could seem like a nut. Please don't take offense, I mean that honestly. I'll start with customs and traditions that would look strange to Americans, then I'll try to show how some American customs are, in two words, out there.

Starting with the viewpoint from the States, there's a place in Scotland where a bride is "blackened" when her family, friends, and possibly enemies cover her with refuse. Sticky stuff, like overripe tomatoes being lovingly tossed at bad stage performers.

In Indonesia, there's a place where a newly married couple won't use the bathroom for three days and nights. Just writing that makes my belly ache, and it doesn't seem helpful for the processes of consummation.

R.L. George

In one East Indian ritual, babies are dropped off a 50 foot temple. They're caught in a cloth stretched tightly below them. Aside from, "What kind of lunacy is this?" and "There's an act of faith, for ya," additional questions and comments come to mind. Two examples are, "I wonder if those babies have more flying dreams than other people?," and "When an Indonesian and an East Indian marry, all they would get for their suffering while trying to consummate the marriage is a baby that gets tossed away." Holy cow, Brahmin!

The last odd other-country custom I'll mention is in the Philippines, where people literally carry their homes with them when they relocate. I guess that isn't so different from American "tiny homes," and that brings me to U.S. traditions that raise international eyebrows.

Americans eat gigantic portions. I once heard about a Chinese menu that stated, to the effect of, "Family dinner. Feeds 10 Chinese or 4 Americans."[70] The amount of food we eat inspires awe in people of different nations, even the other First World countries.

Taxes may be a thing in most countries, but in the U.S., we don't add details about taxes until it's time to pay. So, some Dutch guy tells an American car dealer, "I'll take this new Jetta for $20,000." The dealer says, "It's a great bargain! That'll be $23,000." The Dutch guy might respond, understandably, "*Vat de hel?*"[71] In many other countries, taxes are built into the price. What you see is what you pay.

Lastly—meaning the last thing I'll bring up on the topic of how we're viewed, not the last thing we find weird about one another—is something I personally witnessed. It was a roflmao

---

70 I can't find the source of that menu anywhere. Maybe it was while I was out with a group of five friends, and we had to order two family dinners.
71 The loose English translation is, "Huh?"

moment experienced by a woman from Germany when she saw that wee babies on an American beach were dressed in teeny tiny bathing suits. Which, when thinking about what "roflmao" stands for, I realize the beach reference should change it to "roblmao."

The German woman explained that Europeans don't bother clothing their babies for swimming. Full disclosure (as it were): I don't know if this information is correct, or perhaps the standards have changed since I heard it, but that was one of the first times I realized that we can look a bit tetched to people from other countries.

And as I've said before, we can also look inside and feel nervous about the nature of our own thoughts. "Can my coworkers tell that I'm not wearing any underpants? Do I embarrass myself by flossing[72] in restaurant bathrooms? Should I admit to my addiction to reality television? Are my circling thoughts a sign of mental crumbling?"

Live long, learn about how everyone else is having the same doubts, and you'll be rest assured that there's nothing especially crumbly about your mentality.

I have a theory about a style of thinking, I call it a "capable mind." Those with a capable mind have two qualities. One is they truly understand what they learn, and the other is they're able to continue learning no matter how much education they receive, and no matter how long they live.

It sounds simple because it is. Everybody reading this has gone to school at some point, be it public, private, or home-schooling, so we all know what it is to grasp information that's taught, learn life lessons, and so on. But *understanding* what we've learned isn't a given.

Interestingly, it can also go in the other direction. One

---

72 Dental not dancing

can "understand" better than "learn." That happened to me with algebra. I understand what's going on with equations well enough to get into reading books about physics, but I have had (and still have) trouble *learning* fundamental algebra (and statistics). That's a different type of topic, though.

Back to understanding what we've learned, one of my gripes about how we teach is the approach of "listen and regurgitate."[73] Memorization. "This war was fought in that country between the years seventeen-something and..."

What do we learn about war with that kind of arid info? It's hard to say how well we've absorbed the more profound elements of war, such as the implication of Churchill's observation, "History is written by the victors."

As preposterous as this sounds, we as a human race didn't quite comprehend PTSD until the past 100 years or so, despite having been a warring species from the start of civilization.

It took thousands of years to understand what we've learned over. and over. and over. First, we know that wars happen, but we must understand that it's hard to trust the narratives provided by the winners. Second, wars produce heroes and glory and honor at the cost of alarmingly disordered survivors.

The human race will not evolve without profound understanding. That's the first part of my capable mind theory, and the second part is the ability to continue acquiring and understanding new information. That's a facet of what I'm talking about. When one understands learning, one is able to better appreciate the fact that new information will continually come along. Follow threads of thought for as long as you can,

---

[73] My "no whining about the state of education" algorithm appears to have a glitch.

and I can personally attest that you may never find an end to them.

I know of people who wouldn't necessarily be considered to have genius IQs, but they have such capable minds that I'd take their advice and input more readily than I would the suggestions of a genius. It's sort of like the concept of overcoming a disabling addiction, where if I were a heroin addict or alcoholic, I wouldn't turn to some MD or PhD for help. I would want to be helped by someone who not only learned about overcoming the addiction, but understood the process in an intimate fashion.

Aside from the wonders of a capable mind, there's also "state of mind" to consider. For example, walking into work every day with the mantra, "I'm going to get fired" is dangerous – you may get what you accidentally wish for. Or if you're thinking, "This will make me fat" every time you take a bite of food, common sense dictates that is *not* conducive to losing weight.

Obsessing about negative outcomes can spin other areas of life into unnecessary turmoil. A psychological preoccupation can lead to physical challenges, because there is undoubtedly a connection between the mind and body. I believe at least 51% of physical health is mental health. Instead of telling yourself, "This will make me fat" while you're eating, say, "I'm getting excellent exercise" each time you walk up a flight of stairs.

I recommend careful attention to what you keep at the forefront of your mind, because it can be as obvious as a banner on your forehead. We humans read each other well. Intuition is more strongly associated with women in American society, but men have equal levels.

Speaking of evolution, we'll know the human race is growing when every man is allowed to exhibit the entire range of emotions without being called wimpy.

Everyone has the capacity to intuit what's going on. For example, we all have the ability to sense another's self-loathing like a toxic breeze against our skin. Resist the urge to berate yourself, because others will instinctively suspect there must be a reason to berate you. When you're aware of how a negative self-image can radiate outward, it can help you to dial it back. You have your own instinctual knowledge because *you* can tell when someone else is down on himself.

As much as a spot-on gut-hit can be trusted, the human brain is another source of great power. I can go into a more positive vein for that example. For instance, I've noticed that people who exercise regularly concentrate on the areas of their bodies that are benefiting from the workout. When they do that, they get better results. How could that be? It's mental attention given to physical activity.

A friend once asked me, "Why are you in better shape than I am? All you do is sit around typing all day, then you do about 20 minutes of aerobics-type exercise in the evenings. I work all day at a physically demanding job, I constantly move around. I climb stairs and crawl through attics until I'm out of breath, so I must be getting a cardio workout, right?"

Kind of.

This relates to my idea that "51% of physical health is mental health." While on the job my friend was focused on his work, not the workout. He never took note of which muscles were engaged while he climbed stairs or through attics (he did a lot of wiring in homes and businesses). And when he started breathing heavily because of the energy he expended, he was more likely to think, "I'm tired," rather than, "Hey, that was a nice workout!"

Also, he did not think about the breath moving in and out of his body.

Myth of Normal

I know that statement sounds awfully silly, considering that every living person is going to breathe even if they never think about it, not once. Why bother paying attention to breath?

There's a big answer to that one. Since time immemorial, cultures that use meditation to maintain physical and mental health have recommended noticing and concentrating on breathing. I'll call it "breathing consciousness," with the understanding that others have surely labeled it that way, too. The term is unique to my own mind.

The human body has many automatic functions, including the heartbeat and processes like evacuating the bladder or bowels. It's quite difficult to control the former, and as far as the latter... Well, many who require adult diapers, or laxatives, can testify on those topics.

We *can* control our breath. Pregnant women attend classes (often with male partners) that discuss the importance of certain styles of breathing during childbirth. Yoga and martial arts instructors teach the value of conscious breathing. With that knowledge, those who have never meditated in their lives can improvise and find a bit of peace from poisonous. viral thoughts that loop through their minds (i.e., "Am I going to lose my job? Am I too fat? Will my spouse divorce me?")

Hyperventilation can cause people to pass out; when they're unable to find the strength to breathe calmly, they're told to breathe into a paper bag. Yes, it's backed by a scientific theory,[74] but in my opinion it draws attention to breathing, and that's the biggest reason it helps.

In few, breathing consciousness, or breathing awareness, can reduce stress.

---

74 Hyperventilation can cause a plunge in the body's carbon dioxide, and breathing into a bag is thought to return that $CO2$ to the bloodstream.

R.L. George

Please resist the powers of stress with all your might.

The thing about stress is that it can come at you from any direction. Including, and possibility especially, from the inside. It can feel overwhelming to think about how most of us are within a month or two of poverty at any given moment, or a life-changing accident can happen. That style of thinking gives stress a leg up, or the upper hand.

Seeds of stress can germinate. There you are, relieved because you survived a difficult surgery or you were given a raise at work. Your life seems at least momentarily fine, but the seeds of stress start to sprout, seemingly out of nowhere. "That surgery could have left me crippled," or, "That wasn't as much of a raise as I needed."

You try to relax by chillin' in front of the TV, but mistakenly choose to watch the news. "Say," whispers the stress-monster, "that sword-rattling between those nuclear-capable countries is pretty disturbing." Or, "What's ho? A local alert? What does that color of alert mean? Some little kid has been stolen from her parents?"

Then, you open your door to a knock, and a guy says, "By law, I need to inform you that I am now living two doors down from you..."

In your heightened state of tension you may punch the guy in the throat and end up facing a lawsuit. With a calmer state of mind, you realize that due to your raise, you'll be able to relocate.

Anxiety will rise up within us, or be thrust upon us by the world. It is painful for the mind, body, emotions, and spirit, but we cannot let it become dominant in our way of being. Resist stress from the inner sources, and it will be more bearable when external forces swing toward your knees like a two-by-four.

I see now that the most appropriate closing words on

this topic are if one wishes to maintain her sanity, she must take charge of her stress. Think about your breathing when you're scared, sad, hurt, or angry. Don't worry about the state of your sanity, but if you do, know that it's a good sign to pose that question. Psychopaths never think they're insane.

Bear in mind that "different" doesn't mean "crazy."

Also remember that your thoughts may not align with the ideas of others, but that doesn't mean you're wrong.

Chapter 21:

Warning: This Chapter is NOT Politically Correct

My favorite political orientation is:
the common sense.
— Rodolfo Peon

A while back I lost a beloved friend named Ever Lague. He was told he had two years to live, but he lived another twenty before he died. How did that happen? Could the original doctors have been so wrong?

Aside from the sad truth that doctors can, indeed, be wrong, Ever had a way about him. The best way to describe it is he listened to his body and trusted his senses.

Where's the association with the title of this chapter? Ever smoked cigarettes. Yes, those evil burning sticks that were once between everybody's lips, but are now seen as the scourge of American society. Somehow, despite having a barely measurable immune system, Ever smoked cigarettes, and they are not what killed him. They had nothing to do with what killed him.

I should try to put this into a better context. A few years before I met Ever, I was working with a man named Mike. Mike's father had been sick, and a doctor said, "Your weight, your smoking, and drinking is all going to kill you. If you continue, I won't guarantee that you'll live another two years."

Mike's father lost 50 pounds, stopped smoking and drinking, and within *one* year, Mike's father died. Apparently the stress of trying to flip and spin his lifestyle inside-out did

Myth of Normal

him in.

Now, back to my vignette about Ever. One day, about ten years after he was told he had only two more to go, he asked his doctor, "Do you think I should quit smoking?" His doctor shut the door of the exam room, turned to Ever, and said, "No. Don't change a thing. Whatever you're doing is keeping you alive."

Why a doctor thought that should be kept secret is beyond me.

At various times in my life I've heard interviews of people who have lived 100 years or more. More often than not, they've spoken of habits like taking a shot of whiskey each morning, smoking cigars or cigarettes, or eating bacon every day of their lives. There are residents Shouguang, China— reportedly the most polluted city in the whole wacky world— who live long, relatively sickness-free lives.

Why are particular ways of life deadly to some people, but life-lengthening for others? The opposite also occurs. A non-smoking rural teetotaler who sustains a perfect weight and eats nothing but the healthiest foods dies at age 32.

In my own theory about what happens with the situations I've described above, every human body is so different that we cannot create a set a universal rule for everyone. In other words, it could be a better idea to let your body establish what's normal for you, rather than get eager or antagonistic about health fads or general norms.

It's a shame that we're born with varying abilities to deal with stress, because as I blatantly stated in the previous chapter, stress kills. "But wait!" someone might cry out, "People can be taught to handle stress!" Yes, that's true. However, if a person has no predisposition for hiking through the woods or learning how to meditate, those tools aren't very helpful.

Evidently, Mike's father is someone who fought against

stress with food, alcohol, and cigarettes. My friend Ever certainly used cigarettes to relax, and his doctor must have intuitively concluded that removing that style of relaxation could stress a very sick body past its survival point. Ever lived an additional 10 years after his doctor said, "Don't stop smoking." A total of 20 years passed after his medical death sentence.

Back in the 1940s through the 1960s, people who didn't smoke cigarettes were considered abnormal. Smoking was prescribed, at times, by doctors. Those who were naturally non-smokers were oh-so-relieved to learn that tobacco was a poison that should be erased from the planet!

On the other hand, if smoking really is the killer it's described to be, how are there so many senior-smoker-citizens alive today? I don't mean those who are on commercials discussing all the diseases they're dealing with because of their habit. I mean the 100-year-old lady sitting outside a hut in a Third World country enjoying a home-rolled, non-filter cig.

My own mother smoked a few packs per day during each of her four pregnancies, and not one of us was born disabled (unless "neurotic" is a counted as a disability).

I'm sure there are millions of people who would cringe to read the opening pages of this chapter, and that's why part of its title is a warning.

Now, I must hasten to add that I am not advocating smoking cigarettes as advisable, medically or recreationally. Smoking cannot be found anywhere on any list of good ideas – unless, I guess, one is Native American.

I don't hesitate to make the full-throated recommendation to anyone who cares to listen, "Never, ever start smoking." Why? Because it really does make a lot of people sick, and people do die from smoking.

The same can be said for drinking alcohol. I've seen

Myth of Normal

studies that claim in a worldwide measure, alcohol abuse kills as many people as smoking tobacco. Grain of salt, but still. Common sense.

Setting aside life or death, what about quality of life? How many people have their lives ruined by alcohol? I can't imagine how high that number must be. Where does that fit into the equation of cigarette versus alcohol issues?

Although cigarettes are being phased out in the States, the attempt to illegalize alcohol failed. Besides, like fine cigars, there's something to be said for using (not abusing) fine wines and liqueurs.[75] It's hard to know where to draw the line.

While researching one of my academic essays I learned that obesity—not cigarettes or alcohol—is what takes first place in preventable causes of death in the U.S.. Earlier in this book I expressed my relief that we can't be told to stop eating. Our society does need to address the obesity problem, but ooh, that's a slippery issue. Lack of food is deadly.

We've seen signs of society's proposed solution, such as higher taxes on fattening foods. For all we know, it could get to the point of food addicts holding people up for money so they can buy a fix of fries. There will be dealers preying on the chocoholics, and cheese-pushers will whisper temptations from alleyways. Well, wait, cheeses already whisper from the dairy case, "Yeah, I'm $50 an ounce but man, I am the *best*!"

Another strange phenomenon is the amount time it has taken to start talking smack about our beloved gas-powered automobiles. This is unbelievable because gas-powered cars are much, much more poisonous than tobacco. I once witnessed a woman sitting in a car that had black smoke pouring out of its tailpipe, and she yelled at a smoker waiting at

---

75 Unlikely as it sounds, I believe it is not uncommon for people to be addicted to wine without being alcoholics. Ask a connoisseur.

a stoplight on a bicycle, "You're polluting our world!"

I wonder if that woman ever switched over to an electric car, seeing as how she was so het up about pollution. And even though we are now trying to transition to electric cars, few people care to hear the simple request, "Drive less often."

Cigarette smokers are condemned by people who put 100 miles per day on their gas-powered cars. Yet if one had to choose between staying a week in a sealed garage with ten smokers, or staying one hour in a sealed garage with a single running car...

Most know that a person wouldn't last an hour in a sealed, one-car garage if a car is running while they're in there. Bizarrely, ten smokers surrounding a non-smoker in a sealed garage for a whole week wouldn't damage the average non-smoker. I once knew a cocktail waitress who had worked in bars throughout the 1950s and 1960s, and she smoked cigarettes, herself. When I knew her she was in her 80s, and there wasn't so much as a rasp in her voice.[76]

Addiction is no laughing matter, but is it any less painful to have our freedom stripped away like red, white, and blue paint from a flag?

I do understand the power of commercial television and social media swaying minds, and it is "in" to be anti-bad-habits. Gradual and/or abrupt decreases in freedom is a well-studied embarrassment for humans, but grass-roots and government-seeded propaganda, along with peer-pressure, still works.

If humans are repeatedly told that something is bad for them they tend to try and change their ways. The problems arise when the propaganda isn't exactly honest.

In various eras, we've been led to believe there's evil behind natural sexual tendencies, ranging from masturbation to

---

[76] Incidentally, she also spent her retirement sipping brandy-spiked tea.

Myth of Normal

homosexuality to the act of sex itself. I know that many individuals and entire factions have attempted to follow their society's rules, even when they instinctively disagreed, but what happens next?

Drinkers continue to drink, smokers continue to smoke, and human beings continue to engage in sexual behaviors. They simply hide it from others. It could mean jail time if they're caught, but they're not able or willing to change who they are.

Boy oh boy, that is stressful. Hiding from others, and in some cases hiding from oneself, oof. We'll turn into a bunch of walking time-bombs if our culture keeps trying to illegalize everything.

This is bound to sound irrational to quite a few readers, but I try to avoid voting for laws against problems like smoking tobacco or marijuana. I won't vote for laws that restrict the types of foods people should be allowed to eat. I would never vote to illegalize alcohol. Aside from my passion for wine, my voting behaviors are based on a single concept.

If I vote for a law that takes something away from others, the next law that gets voted in might take something away from *me*.

Impossible? Let's hope this overpopulated world doesn't start suggesting a law that limits the number of children each couple can have.[77] Who would vote for such a thing, you may ask. Sadly, everybody who gets swayed by the propaganda would vote for it. And if they don't, some powerful person might go ahead and mess with the vote count to get whatever it is they want, anyway. No more big families.

Sigh, such a world. It makes me feel some empathy for everyone who smokes and drinks and eats too much. And

---

77 Sounds insane? Ask citizens of China if it could happen.

even though I think it's a terrible idea to continue overpopulating this world, I would never vote for a law that tells people they cannot have kids.

Chapter 22: Rascally Children

*If you want your children to listen,
try talking softly to someone else.*
— Ann Landers

Kids don't miss a thing. We think we're hiding our bad habits from them, but all we're doing is modeling the bad habit of underestimating the observational powers of children.

Back when I was a youngster I heard that old saw, "Don't mind his grumpiness, he doesn't like kids." I was bewildered. "How confusing," I thought. "I've heard about not liking people who are different, but *everyone* has been a kid!"

We forget. As an adult, a thick hedge in the yard looks like work. It needs to be watered and trimmed. For kids, it's a hiding place. An adult purchases a big stereo or TV and has to figure out the best way to dispose of the carton, but a kid repurposes it into a fort. Or in the case of a flat-screen TV box, a sled.

It can be pretty fun to watch how kids do things. Some behaviors inspire hope in the parents. We tend to look for future professions, like a baby keeping a beat with a wooden spoon is a future musician, or the little girl who takes apart and puts together retractable pens is a future engineer.

But. In terms of what is a normal versus an abnormal child, that can get downright scary. It's so hard to understand why they're the only one among their friends who didn't like that movie, or couldn't play that one game. How frightening, to feel like your kid is the odd kid out. Parents find themselves looking at their overly withdrawn or wildly rambunctious young'uns and asking, "What is wrong with them? Are all kids like that? Is my kid a wacko?"

Tantrums are a good example of unnerving child behavior.

When one of my countless nieces and nephews was about 7 years old, we were taking a walk on the beach. On the way home she started sulking about something, and then stopped walking. We had to get home, but I couldn't talk her into walking a step further.

I was a very young adult at the time, and I tried pleas, demands, even threats, "Wait until your parents hear about this!" I bargained with her, I also tried some emotional blackmail, "This is bummin' me out, kiddo!" When I tried to pick her up she let out a shriek, which produced the desired result – I set her down. What else could I do? I sat down next to her.

Patience was my only possible response. I sat there on that beach walkway and apologized to those who stepped around us. The rest of my time was invested in contemplating whether my niece had some kind of mental disability that was starting to show up at age 7.

Nope. She was being a kid, that's all.

Everything I'm saying about this is outside the scope of a child that *does* have a medical condition. What I'm focused on is the way kids can seem cray-cray, but not when you're comparing them with other kids. And we must resist comparing them to adults, because if we threw ourselves to the floor wailing about the price of cheese in a grocery store, the authorities would be called.

Children can act strange and goofy and they can show distinct signs of insanity, but they're about as normal as anything can be in our cockamamie world.

It wouldn't surprise me to learn that if there are sentient

Myth of Normal

aliens out there, they develop differently than humans. They'd probably think that right from the start, our way of entering life is pretty freaky. Picture it. You're pulled out of a warm, safe environment, and the first thing to happen is someone makes you cry. Sure, the point is to get you to start breathing, but hey, hello, ow.

For the most part we're able to communicate as soon as we're born, but the grownups in charge often have trouble understanding us. We then learn to speak their language with our words, bodies, and expressions. We grow to know that there are "normal" ways of interacting.

If we want to easily get along, we follow the norms. If we want to make a splash, we float above the bubble and dance outside the box. We lead.

Which would you want your child to do? I imagine the reactions to that question start with "Of course..." However, a preference for offspring that will float and dance—and possibly lead—is sadly not a given. I once saw a Twitter comment that said to the effect of, "I tweet crazy things in order to sabotage any hope of my child becoming a politician." Funny, yes, but also telling. A person has to be nuts to become a politician, while a grounded white-collar worker might be sheltered from the irrationalities of governance.

On the other side of the fence, having children who get along easily (perhaps boringly) is not everyone's greatest hope. There are parents who will do everything in their power to make sure their children will climb into that special stratosphere of power.

The good news/bad news is that we can try to guide the young toward what we insist is the right way to live, but off they go with their own ideas. It's up to you to decide which part of that is good news, and which is bad news.

In the meantime, our best hope is to talk to young

people. We never know how they'll respond until they do, which means we also must listen. Actively listening to children helps us to understand them, and besides, we're also teaching them. We're modeling how good it feels to be heard!

Chapter 23: Whose script is this, anyway?

> *"If you expect nothing from somebody you are never disappointed."*
> – Sylvia Plath

One of the most embarrassing things that can happen is to say to someone, for the first time, "I love you," and there's no reply. The best declarations of love are made with no motivation beyond saying it aloud, but the most satisfying followup is to hear, "I love you too." Well, it's usually satisfying. When that response feels scripted it can sting.

As much as we'd like to insist otherwise, we have a boatload of expectations every time we speak and listen. It happens to me when I'm reading, too. I'll get to the bottom of the right hand page, and it's in the middle of a sentence. When I turn the page, I'm already zipping on because I've guessed what the next word will be.

When the next word is not what I expected I feel a tingle of appreciation for the author. Please, surprise me! Like when a sentence begins, "He jumped up and —", turn the page expecting "down" but instead it says, "up and up." Or, "It was a dark and stormy —", and the sentence finishes with, "thought."

Think of the number of times you started a conversation that accidentally turned into an argument. You say something, the response is so unexpected that you repeat, paraphrase, or try to explain your side of it. The other person didn't see that coming, and so steps into the same but separate circle of repeating, paraphrasing, or explaining her own take on the subject.

Neither of you are following the other's script. It's frustrating.

Our word choices can get us into trouble, too. I once whispered to someone who was behaving in an unacceptable manner, "Your behavior is insufferable." He was so infuriated that his fists bunched up. Whatever association he had with the word "insufferable" made it sound much worse than what I meant, which was "unreasonable." (He'd been having a fit of temper in a public setting.)

Now that I've written about that I'm wondering what he would have thought if I had used the word "churlish,"[78] which I now realize is the most suitable adjective for his behavior that day. Knowing him, he would have heard "girlish," and then pretended he was wearing a ponytail while he offered a curtsy. I miss that knucklehead's inability to understand me.

No matter who we are and where we live we're all actors caught up in performing the play, movie, or video, reading scripts that are carefully edited by external entities. This is life as a being in the human race. Fortunately there's another aspect of performing on the great stage of this world: we can write our own scripts.

Those who are chasing a dream of normality are the ones who stolidly follow their role during the drama, and when comedy raises its blessed head, they contribute to the laugh-track. They dutifully read their lines, but they're often stymied when the other actors start to improvise.

You are not the only one who has been startled by improv. You yourself have probably strayed from the plot now and again. "Sorry Mom, I don't want to be a doctor. No, Dad, becoming a wife is not my life's ambition." Do you remember their bewildered expressions when you spoke your truth? You

---

78 Ill-mannered

wear the same expression when someone else speaks against the truths that you hold onto.

It isn't only you, it's not specific to your country, it happens in every single family and society.

I'm obviously a fan of words, both by nature and by the nurture of having parents who enjoyed talking about words. Mombo was a poet who could get full-on irritable about incorrect pronunciation or made-up words. "It isn't a cupboard, it's pronounced like 'cubberd.' And 'lawyer' should be said 'law-yer,' not 'loy-er.'"

"Mombo," I rejoined, "it depends on where you come from. For 'oregano' we say 'oh-RAY-gah-no,' but the British say, 'oh-ray-GAH-no.' In fact, their way makes sense to me because of the way we pronounce the word 'origami.'"

Our conversation went off for a few minutes into the wonderland of various languages, including British versus American English, Japanese, and Italian.[79] When we got back to the way of English words, Mombo started grumbling about new ones, like "ginormous" and "conversate."[80]

"'Conversate' is not a word," Mombo complained. "Why do people keep using it?"

"It's the same reason words are pronounced in different ways by different English speakers. English is *alive*. It's a living language. A hundred years ago nobody knew anything about a dramedy, foodies, or blogs."

I then interjected that if I'd had any say in it, I'd have found a better word than "blog." It's fun to make up words, ask Shakespeare if you meet him in the afterlife. I've been

---

79 In Italian oregano is *origano*, and the pronunciation would sound American if it weren't spoken with an Italian accent.
80 My spellcheck recognizes "ginormous," but not "conversate." Nor does it recognize "spellcheck." Spellcheckers (a word that's incongruously accepted by my spellcheck program) must have trouble keeping up.

trying to get *e-dress* to replace *email address* for about seven years, now, which makes me think "e-log" would have been a better choice than "blog."

Anyway. Mombo had to agree with my reasoning about English being a living language, but she didn't have to like certain growth spurts.

Pop, her ex of 50 years, didn't like what people did with some words, either. One of his pet peeves was when someone said "member" when they meant, "*re*member." He developed the annoying habit of pointing it out whenever someone said it, and then correcting them with those italics in the first two letters of the word.

I found a way to stop him by pointing out that he said "prolly" when he meant "probably." That observation got under his skin, and he became so distracted by paying attention to how he pronounced his own words that he lost confidence in griping about "member."

It's easy to pick at others about how they speak until we notice our own errors. However, shutting people up (or shutting them down) is not a nice goal. I think allowing others their own words and pronunciation is a strong initial step toward proper communication.

A second step is to avoid writing a script before, during, or after a conversation. A third step is to resist becoming angry when other(s) don't dutifully speak the lines you had assigned to them.

My final suggestion is to have courage. In its way, improv is a lot more challenging than a production with scripted dialogue, props, direction, and practiced acting. If nothing else, it's quite a bit more real.

Myth of Normal

Chapter 24: Creativity (the inexhaustible stuff of living)

> *In the world of normal*
> *originality is a superpower.*
> – R.L. George

Soon, this Commonsense Series will include a book about the importance of creativity. I'm so beguiled by the topic that I'm not able to resist giving it a bit of space here.

The quote that opens this chapter is my own, although I considered Jung's observation, "Normality is a fine ideal for those who have no imagination." I also thought about Maya Angelou's gem, "If you are always trying to be normal, you will never know how amazing you can be."

Where does imagination come from? Is it possible for a person who's not inspired to be amazing?

Creativity, imagination, inspiration, these human qualities are priceless. I don't use the word "superpower" lightly, but there it is. Creativity has power, and by "super" I mean "exceptional." I once academically defined creativity with two words: "Remarkably original."

It would be easier to list situations where creativity wouldn't work rather than how many ways it can be helpful, but I'm not one to take the easy way out. First I'll say that in general, one need only think of the extraordinarily creative people who add to our world. Musicians, writers, painters, actors, all of them are reaching us in a way that help us to make sense of the transcendent moments, or the dark cold ugly facets of life.

Musicians with messages can reach a larger audience than national leaders. The same is true of authors, but I really was wowed when the musician Bob Dylan won the Nobel Prize in literature. Another example of a mixed talent like that is Di Vinci. What an astonishing imagination!

When it comes to plays and movies, wow. The writers, directors, set designers, and of course the actors have given us creations that are as real as life itself. Movies can change lives and yes, even reestablish norms. That includes fiction and non-fiction presentations.

Science and history are filled with creativity. By "science" I'm not referring to science fiction, but that's a good point on its own. Few have failed to notice how much our current technology reflects fantastical inventions by authors like Jules Verne and Gene Roddenberry. In any event, scientists can stare at statistics all they like, but how does one have an "ah-ha" moment if she has no imagination?

Scientists are a lot like non-fiction authors, because they gather information and put it into what is (hopefully) a readable and understandable form. A very good scientist will find a way to interest or entertain the world with her discoveries. This is how I feel.

With regard to history, there's a creative element in retelling events that aren't exactly the truth. Published lies about history is a galactic betrayal of the human race, but it is an artistic talent.

Another facet of creativity in history is something I alluded to above, when I mentioned the way creative artists can reach us. Writers and musicians, painters and sculptors from the past have given us another way of seeing into their world.

The Terracotta Army leaps to mind. Emperor Qinshihuang's Mausoleum is filled with thousands of soldiers (among other figures), all of them with finely honed characteristics. That alone is awesome, but I remember one time while watching a camera pan along the ranks of terracotta soldiers, I noticed a lone scamp leaning out of line wearing a playful expression.

Creativity, wow. More than 2,000 years ago, a whole bunch of artists were involved in making that massive terracotta army, which included the rascally soldier. These ancient human beings and their creation help us apprehend the strand that runs through us all, through time. We've always had a capacity for art, hard work, and humor. And the playful soldier reminded me of how each and every war has been filled with regular people.

My imagination can sweep me away at any given moment. It did just that in the above paragraph. My brain made transitions from a historical mausoleum to an individual soldier, and then to the focus of regular people who fight in wars. There's a story in there somewhere – well, there are stories everywhere.

How did Emperor Qinshihuang's soldiers live before they were conscripted or talked into joining the military? The playful soldier obviously has a sense of humor, which makes him special. If instead of sculptures the army had been photographed, that one guy would hold up rabbit ears behind someone's head, and a higher-up thinks, "I'm going to have to keep a close eye on him."

Playful soldier gets noticed. He could have come from extreme poverty, but improbably rises to the rank of general in the otherwise oligarchical military. His life is enhanced by his divergent way of thinking.

Imagination, it can save you, for instance it will keep you on alert while you're walking through threatening woods or a concrete jungle. Coming up with counteractions or escape routes requires the ability to creatively envision various scenarios that will help you in an emergency.

Your imaginative faculties are a part of every process

that starts with questions, like "I wonder if?" or "What if?" An example is, "I wonder if I should propose to her? What if she says yes?"

Pondering a proposal of marriage engages long-term fantasies. Sharing a living space day after month after year, possibly filling that space with children, hopefully you'll be together for the rest of your lives. Your marriage will be a success, your family will conquer obstacles and endure life's trials, you can see it all before you propose to your beloved.

Creative exploration is nearly constant. While we live each day on earth, virtual reality is alive and dancing through our minds. Imagination remains active even while we sleep. It's the stuff of magic.

Needless to say, there's also a dark side.

Sometimes the imagination is spooky. Fantasizing about death and/or destruction can be blood chilling. It isn't as abnormal as one would think, though. We watch so many movies about death and destruction that it's a trillion-dollar industry, all told. However, every producer will beg fans of violent movies, "Please do not try this at home."

One must be careful of imagining the worst that can happen because it can become a self-consuming snake. That circling dread can eat you alive. "I'll never get married, I can see myself old and alone. What if my boss fires me, how will I survive?"

Thoughts of doom are manufactured via the exact same brainwork that goes into fun fantasies. If someone genuinely believes he'll never get married, for whatever reasons, he can channel his visualizations in a more hopeful direction. For example, "not married" does automatically lead to "alone." Blood relatives and chosen family are such satisfying relationships. Also, this is a little known fact,[81] but marriage

Myth of Normal

and children are very time-consuming. Imagine, imagine, imagine what you could do with all the additional time provided by singledom!

Seriously. I've heard people say they don't have a creative bone in their body, and I always wholeheartedly disagree. Just because you're not a musician or writer or painter, that doesn't mean you're not the creative type. What I'm saying is every average individual has the capacity to make something that's wholly unique, and solve problems with inspired thinking.

For those who do have the itch to create what is specifically art, please give it a scratch. If your muses are jumping but you're sitting still, your spirit could... I don't know, seize up. Atrophy. You can get all jammed up inside, and that is not emotionally or psychologically healthy. In fact, if you're worried that you're stuck in any kind of void, and it feels abnormally unhealthy, it might help to talk to a psychologist.

---

81 That's sarcasm.

R.L. George

Chapter 25: The Psychology of Normal

*Normality is
the Great Neurosis of civilization.*
– Tom Robbins

Tom Robbins may not have been a psychologist, but he sure did make an insightful observation about normality. The discipline of psychology disagrees with what he said, but that could be because they're still trying to apply statistics to human behavior.

Defining abnormal is hard enough, never mind normal. An older man goes to a young therapist and complains of an irresistible urge to cry during sad movies. The therapist scratches her head because she doesn't see that as a problem, but her patient does. Or, a young man goes to an older therapist concerned about *not* being able to cry during sad movies. The older therapist scratches his head...

The challenge of drawing tidy boxes around indicators of general normality and abnormality comes back to subjectivity. Both patients would have to be asked, "Is this unusual behavior for *you?*"

That's key to the whole point of this book: in a world of billions there are billions of opinions on what's zany and what's not. The best judge of whether anything is askew in your everyday life is you.

According to a variety of sources, the weight of the average U.S. citizen is... overweight. Yes, it's normal to be overweight. That being the case, who'd want to be like everyone else?

It isn't normal, on the other hand, to win a Nobel Prize.

Myth of Normal

Who wouldn't want to be an outlier on *that* bell curve?

I know, the reason we have a bell-shaped curve at all is because someone is counting heads and manipulating data, but still. If you're not winning international prizes you may still be one of a handful who can balance the edge of a coin in the part of your hair. That's a neat trick! You're special.

"Different" and "special" are often interchangeable. It isn't commonplace to be the life of every party, and those people are seen as special. It's more common to feel a little nervous at social gatherings, but nobody really wants to be that guy or gal. Sliding down the curve of discomfort to the extreme of social anxiety is where it gets unbearable.

Physical symptoms of social anxiety include sweating, trembling, and blushing so fiercely that onlookers worry about your blood pressure. Psychological symptoms are even worse, with overwhelming fear topping the list.

Another of those vicious, self-consuming snake situations arises. Those with social anxiety fear they'll do something embarrassing or humiliating, like trembling in public or sweating profusely. When that person enters a social situation with circling thoughts, such as, "I will not panic," it puts panic smack at the front of the mind.

It could be one of the most disturbing facets of social anxiety that the sufferer is hyper-aware of the condition occurring. It reminds me of addictive behavior, where people are recognizing, "This is going to kill me" even as they overindulge. How to deal with these issues?

Experts have all sorts of suggestions. In some cases, medication is effective. Or, therapists have encouraged gradual exposure to the scary situations, one step at a time, building an arsenal of responses to the arising fears.[82]

---

82 Cognitive Behavior Therapy

My gut tells me it's also a matter of rewriting one's internal dialogue. A key issue of social anxiety is that self-consciousness is seen as excessive, but what if it's only commendable carefulness?

I've always been impressed by those who pause and think before responding in a conversation. I don't have that kind of patience. To be self-conscious can mean avoiding saying the wrong thing, as long as it doesn't result in saying nothing at all.

Many who have social anxiety do soldier through group interactions at work, in school, or other social settings. That is astoundingly brave. Self-kudos for courage! Facing up to a powerful fear, especially without the benefit of therapy,[83] is quite a feat.

Another way of reassessing the threat of socializing is to go all the way back to childhood, when it seemed like everyone in high school was set up for the rest of their lives. "Most likely to" yearbook captions range from, "become a senator" to "rob a bank." I wonder how many times the student said to become a senator grows up to be an actor, or a cop, or a janitor, while the expected thug is voted into office.

What I'm trying to stress is that the way we see others, and are seen by others, will evolve over time. We know that to be true because we have the advantage of *a posteriori* vision. Long after we've graduated, we can look back and see what happened to people after they left the creepy fish-bowl-living of high school.

If I have any readers who are high school students, I promise you, very few people wind up on the path that was prophesied by their peers. That's doesn't have to be a downer for those who were slated for promising careers like acting or

---

83 The majority of people with social anxiety don't seek professional help.

Myth of Normal

politics. It's either a warning (i.e., avoid temptations that can derail you), or it's a reassurance that *you* will be the one to figure out what it is you want to do with your life.

When it comes down to it, buying into a scientific psychological definition of normality is no safer than accepting everything written in history books as God's truth. New developments are continual, just take a look at the Diagnostic Statistician's Manual (DSM), and see what kinds of behaviors were once considered to be mental illnesses.

Female Hysteria. Female Sexual Dysfunction. Homosexuality. Penis Envy. Childhood Bi-Polar Disorder.[84] Or, they could just make a sweeping diagnosis of Personality Disorder. Wow, the nerve of some shrinks! As Curly the Stooge would say, the very noive!

I firmly believe the best way to muddle through this world is to build one's own philosophy.

---

84 If a child had a constant, perfectly smooth personality, I would worry about him.

R.L. George

Chapter 26: The Philosophy of Normal

> *In human behavior,*
> *what is most intriguing*
> *is not the average,*
> *but the improbable.*
> – Martin Seligman

In these pages, I've already talked a bit about the philosophers Nietzsche and Kant. Nietzsche is seen by many as a champion of individualism, while Kant was a proponent of normalization. Both of them had a talent for maxims.

Nietzsche was quite fond of offering pithy pearls of wisdom. Here are a few:

"He who attains his ideal by that very fact transcends it." The relevance to my theme is a bit of a paradox. 1) Your ideal may be outside the norm, like striving for a Nobel Prize. This means if you attain your ideal, you've transcended the cage of society's expectations. 2) If your preferred ideal is to always fit in, achieving that means you've transcended the norms because really, no one fits in with everyone else. You're free to be abnormally normal, deliciously so.

Another Nietzscheism is, "One begins to mistrust very clever people when they become embarrassed." That's just funny.

Yet another: "Two people with the same principles probably seek something fundamentally different with them." Yes, people can be in agreement about a religion, a political party, ethics, etc., and still have different motivations and goals for their beliefs. Seeing as how that is so, norms fly out every open window.

Him again: "There are no moral phenomena at all, only a moral interpretation of phenomena." That one seems to belong in the chapter about ethics and morals, but here it is as one of Nietzsche's philosophies. This is what I'm sayin' about perspective! We're all in an ongoing state of interpreting morality.

Kant was an ethicist, but in contrast to the above quote, he didn't care much for subjectivity. That's what inspired the only maxim he came up with (and in it, he uses the word "maxim"). It's his Categorical Imperative, and I footnoted it earlier: "Act only according to that maxim whereby you can, at the same time, will that it should become a universal law."

There are plenty of arguments about the strength of that statement. Here's an example: Your loved one is dying, and you don't want him to be afraid. You lie and say, "You'll get through this." That would be against Kant's maxim because your action of lying means you think it should be a universal law that lying is, in general, okay.

There are too many situations like that, where lying is wrong "unless." During the past few centuries, thinkers have tried to qualify their acceptance of Kant's Categorical Imperative. For instance, it's never okay to lie unless you need to keep from hurting someone's feelings. Or, only lie if it will stop physical harm from happening to you or someone else. Or, lie if it can forestall a catastrophe. The list is long, especially when it starts getting subjective.

Acts of killing, and killing killers, also exemplify the glitch in the Kantian philosophy. There will always be a contextual factor when it comes to a given culture's attitude about causing the death of another, and by "culture" I include religious and political ideals.

The Bible says, "Thou shalt not kill" and also, "An eye for an eye." Execution of murderers is seen as normal in various countries, and the death penalty is an option in quite a few U.S. states. For those cultures the maxim is if you kill, you'll be killed.

Unless. Unless you're a police officer or a soldier. Unless you killed in self-defense, or you killed someone accidentally.

When gifted with a single wish, it's devious to wish for more wishes. I bring that up because the best use of Kant's maxim is to say, "I will only consider Kant's maxim subjectively, and I can will that to be a universal law."

That's philosophical humor. What I really mean is it would be too complicated to live by the pure Kantian ethics as set forth in his Categorical Imperative. That's why I think it's such a good idea to develop our own philosophies.

With regard to the biggie, that of killing, the number of deadly wars that have scarred our earth show how many agree with taking life as a soldier. That can also be logged as killing in defense. Philosophically, ancient Egyptians espoused justifiable war, and the same is true of East India's *Mahabharata.* Aristotle and Confucius are specific philosophers who argued just wars. What's your opinion, dear reader? Soldiers protect the civilians in their culture from invaders and carnage. If anyone doubts that, propaganda will weave a shroud of political incorrectness around anti-war attitudes. Even as individuals it's hard to disagree with protecting others.

Those who believe no one should kill another human being, ever, are in good company. Conscientious objectors loathe the idea of taking a life, and they actually stand under with the motto, "the right to refuse to kill." Gandhi comes to the forefront of my mind because passive resistance was so startlingly effective. There are many religious factions that will not kill, no matter what the circumstances.

Myth of Normal

Do you agree, reader, that there's never a good enough reason to kill another human being? Personally, I find executions to be based on strange logic. It certainly does seem hypocritical to kill someone in order to make a statement about the sinfulness of killing.

Across the board, from killing to stealing a loaf of bread, from abusing a child to disciplining that child, from loving thy neighbor to being in love with that neighbor, how are we supposed to decide how to think or act?

It's nearly impossible to find universal agreement on normality, much less a consensus on any philosophy of the subject. Pretty silly, considering that normality *requires* a consensus. Is it any wonder that trying to be normal is such a task?

Philosophy belongs to the collective human race more than to big names from history. I am a philosopher[85] who believes we're meant to offer as many questions as answers. The best example is, "Does anybody believe there's such a thing as 'normal'?"

My personal answer is yes, people believe there is such a thing. That's logical. What I find to be a shame is how much energy is spent on trying to *be* normal. Well, unless you're being normal for you.

"The new normal" is a recently popularized concept that speaks volumes to my theory, here. It's quixotic to apply universal ways of thinking and behaving across large numbers of humans. The reason cultures do try to set regulations and social mores is because we're all so different! But if we're going to live together in some semblance of peace, we've got to agree on a few things.

What works for me is to graciously accept the proper

---

[85] By academic degrees, and as an individual

laws of my own society, or of a society I'm visiting. By "laws" I'm referring to legislation that's meant to keep us safe and sane. Otherwise, I'm all for allowing every individual to break out of the box and thrive on a style of freedom that encourages being oneself.

Remember what Jung once said: "I am not what happened to me. I am what I choose to become."

Chapter 27: What's the point of all this?

*To succeed,
jump as quickly at opportunities
as you do at conclusions.*
– Benjamin Franklin

I'm deeply curious about what you, as an individual reader, have concluded from the ideas I've expressed in this book. Disagreement is welcome and encouraged. Complete agreement with everything would be a pleasant surprise, but I admit it would also worry me a little.

Clearly, conformity is not my thing. It comes up in the prologue that I'm abnormal, and I have no qualms about that. The phenomena of subjectivity and perspective are queen and king of anti-normality, in my mind, because for every normal behavior there are a dozen abnormal responses. A way to think about it is that it seems typical for a person to get up and go to a job five days a week, but a surprising amount of people do no such thing. There are studies and statistics about that.

Yeah, statistics. I'm not a fan. The subject always made me uncomfortable as a student, but as a thinker, I do know quantitative analysis has its place. Statistics that are fed to the public, though, can be falsified or purposely misleading. That's off-putting.

As an example, a researcher could say nine out of ten people are overweight, but they recruited participants from fast food restaurants and speed-eating contests. Or, a researcher who loathes religion could tweak his bell-curve when the data shows him that churches actually help people.

When it comes to common sense, ya can't fake it.

What we can do is chuckle at ourselves when we start taking ourselves too seriously. I don't know how many remember the first time they experienced embarrassment, but I'd wager it was during your childhood. A lifetime of looking different or living as *you* choose might make you a target for some teasing, but so be it, laugh along with them if you can. Try not to judge their asininity, lest ye be judged.

Judgmentality is a rough topic because we all need to make the occasional judgment call, yet it's hard to take when we're unfairly assessed by others. We're also capable of picking ourselves to pieces, raking our fingernails across every flaw, and that's to our own detriment. Examine yourself, understand yourself, but try not to judge.

It can be so hard to know how our own standards are viewed by others, particularly those from different cultures. We see them as having outlandish customs, they see us as having bizarre ways, but is anyone right or wrong? Well, yes, but can we blame them, if they've spent their entire lives in their specific culture? There are some U.S. values that others see as pretty loopy, but it's hard for us to see because we're too close to it. The best we can all do in this world is learn as much as we can about each other before we even attempt to make a decision about their weirdness.

Beware of what disturbs you, including feelings about new societal twists like the gender trend. Simplistic black-and-white notions of male/female have begun to blur in the 21st century, and although it can be tempting to resist, change is a-coming. Rather than fight it, I recommend finding solace in your own gender identification – even if it's the b/w M/F version. You know what's right for you, and security in that knowledge makes it easier to accept what's right for someone else.

That applies to more than raising one's eyebrows about

unusual gender identifications, and I think it's the best way to look at everyone who falls into the category of "other." Self-acceptance and self-respect radiate outward and reverberate, and those dispositions are mirrored back. Inevitably, it will come to light that people who are of another race, or LGBTQ, or in a different income bracket, they're all just people.

On an old episode of MASH Corporal Klinger is learning about yoga, and he says, "only through accepting others for what they are will you find true inner tranquility."[86] In other words, if we want to feel good on the inside we can start by accepting what lies outside of us. Otherwise, to assume that anyone is wrong about being who they are... Wow, that's fraught with emotional, spiritual, and intellectual danger.

Feeling anger toward others is even more emotionally stressful. It gives them power over you, because you should be in charge of your own emotions, but there they are "causing" you to feel anger. That's toxic, and it can eat away at your spirit, too. Whether your faith tells you to love your neighbor or love the one you're with, throwing shards of anger or distaste at nonconforming passersby is counterproductive to love.

Pressuring others to be someone other than themselves is also illogical. Thinkers who disagree must ask themselves, "Would I allow anyone to change *my* mind?" If the answer is "no," that illustrates the reason why it's useless to try and change the minds of others. Others can be shamed or shunned, or in extreme cases, incarcerated for the way they think, but none of that changes their minds.

The human mind is a masterpiece, really. Not only can it grasp everything from humor to logic to a higher power, it can also go off on its own private tangents. Dreaming, for instance. Dreams are a safe environment for exploring wishes.

---

[86] Season 11, episode 10.

R.L. George

Or, they offer up visuals of our depths like a movie of the week. Sometimes, they give us a bit of foresight, and other times, they're a total mystery.

It's rare for dreams to follow any strands of normality. During a single night, the dreamer can simultaneously be a child and a grandparent, it can be the 1990s while it's the present day. A week can pass in the space of a night's dream, and then return to the month before as the sun starts to rise in reality. The sources of dreams span from the mystical to the scientific, and I don't think they're anything to fear.

Nightmares are spooky, yes, and yet they still hold messages in the same way regular dreams do. If someone is suffering constant nightmares I would recommend professional help, because it would be hard to deal with that. Fortunately, most of us have basic dreams, and a lot of fun can be found in them. This is especially true of dreams that involve all the senses, including sight, smell, sound, touch, and taste.

Taste. Yes, one of my favorite sleeping adventures involves my most beloved pastime. Eating.

In these pages I spoke of the joys of food, and I thanked the gods and goddesses that be, no one can stop us from eating. It's an unavoidable necessity. I made those comments with the confidence that human beings will always *want* to eat, but then I watched a science documentary about foods for astronauts traveling through space, and I felt the cold splash of a wake-up call. We have no choice but to eat, but what if the only options are unpleasant?

No one can force us to stop eating, but they can give us gruel, or subject us to soylent green,[87] which is like Oliver Twist-flavored gruel. There's a distinct possibility that the human diet will have to change someday, for a variety of

---

87 A 1973 movie. The most famous line: "Soylent green is *people!*"

reasons, but until then, I'll continue to love my current choices.

When it comes to food, "to each their own taste" couldn't be more applicable. Because we must eat to survive, why not make the most of it? There is that bell curve of America's norm of "overweight," but one way to get yourself outside that norm is to genuinely savor every flavor. Prepare foods with attention to subtle details around seasonings, textures, and visuals.[88] That approach is helpful for those who are underweight, too.

Nevertheless, I think it's more important to eat based on tastes rather than using food to try and adjust the way you look. Attractiveness is weighed on a lot more than physical appearance.

The flaws we see in the mirror are rarely visible to others. Conversely, others see beauty you might miss in yourself. A way to get this at the gut level is to think of how you see the people you love. Look at your lovely grandmother, your handsome son, your awesome mom! They can have trouble seeing what you see in them, and the reverse is likely too. It often happens that others can admire your qualities better than you can.

Besides, working on your looks from the outside-in has more pitfalls. Times and tastes change so often that there's no way for everyone to always sustain an *en vogue* appearance. Body size and hairstyles, facial structure and skin tone, clothing fads and so on, it can be hard to keep up. What really makes the striking people gorgeous is their traits.

Charisma, humor, intelligence, kindness, find a respectable quality within your own personality and nurture it. That's what will draw people to you for friendship and love.

---

[88] Though I still argue textures and visuals couldn't possibly apply to jellied moose nose.

Strip away the clothes (preferably in private), age beyond questions of weight, hair, high cheekbones and fresh young skin, and what do you have? Your essential self. Do you still have loved ones? Yes. They chose to know and love you based on you, not your society's opinion of your attractiveness.

Trust that you're lovable, no matter how you look. Just ask Scamp the Tramp, named 2019's ugliest dog. Who can help but love that guy?

Asking you to trust that you're lovable is another way of saying "have faith in yourself."

I know, faith can be quite a chasm to cross. It's blind belief, absolute conviction that what you believe is true, no matter what anyone else says. It isn't specific to religion, either, because people are also righteous about their nation and their own particular politics.

Some religions, nations, and political factions feel that those who disagree are so wrong that they should be killed. Yet among the billions of individuals living on this planet, there are hundreds of millions of belief systems. Those who hold to being Buddhist, or Christian, or Muslim or Shinto or atheist, they aren't about to toss lifelong beliefs and practices because someone says they must.

The same is true of patriotism, which most of us are born into. We're raised to love, respect and prepare to protect our country. It gets burned into our very DNA. Politically, we form our preferences as we go through life, and we also find ourselves subjected to insidious propaganda that could sell steaks to a cow.

It is possible to change a mind now and then, but for the most part, we're best off accepting that others believe differently than we do. Your norms are yours, theirs are theirs. I'm sure hundreds of millions of people would argue this, but there is no great exact-answer machine that can state: "This, and only this, is the correct way to think!" That is why we're left with acceptance, if we want the human race to continue past the 21st century.

Wait, there is another option. Become a world leader. Yes, that's abnormal, as is great wealth. So, we can become deviants by gathering vast power and attempting to establish norms. Otherwise, the only way to fit in and get along is to accept that there is no real "normal."

When I said "become a world leader," above, it sounded flippant. It's actually a big deal. Try to name three of the best world leaders of today, based on who they are and what they're doing with their power. One, maybe two can instantly come to mind, but to come up with three might require a few hours. Look it up online, do you agree with the choices?

If you disagree, or you don't like your *own* national, spiritual, or cultural leaders, that is no surprise. Each country on this planet is filled with individuals who don't feel good about other nations, or they're out of sync with elements of their own culture.

You are one of those individuals. I know how tempting it can be to want to go along with the crowd, to fit in, to feel comfortable among others. Nevertheless, I beg you to stand out, even if it's in your own mind. Rather than feel safe with the thought, "I'm just one of the guys/gals," seek strength in your uniqueness. "I'm perfect as I am. I'm the standard of 'me.' Nobody else can do me better, I am the quintessential _____" (enter your name).

That type of thinking eases the pain of feeling like an outsider, and I am convinced that we'll all find ourselves in that cold place at one time or another. Insider status is fragile and temporary, because in order to remain an insider, individuality is set aside. The inside of a closed system can get stale.

Prison-like.

Which reminds me that I also spoke about crimes and imprisonment in these pages. The topic of guilt was in there, too, but the assignment of guilt isn't the sole decision of courts and societies. We feel guilty all by ourselves, judging and punishing all of our decisions and actions that we've deemed unacceptable.

What I don't understand is people talk themselves to sleep each night by raking over their missteps and mistakes, while criminals in powerful positions around the world are cheating, killing, and making the lives of millions miserable.

We all make mistakes, there is no denying that, but not at the level of those with abnormal wealth and influence. Also, very few people set out to purposely screw up, yet the monstrously powerful really do think about how to addict the masses to medications, or how to steal a country by killing its inhabitants until they submit.

When someone feels guilty about a great personal error, real or imagined, I always recommend checking oneself on a scale of ten. Put the worst human monsters at the top, including names from history, and then work your way down the list of serial killers, rapists, etc. Where are you on that list of sinners? Probably a lot closer to one, like Gandhi or Christ, than you are to a ten of those who attempt the genocide of entire races of people.

The strange thing about that statement is that some essentially regular individuals do think it would be no big deal to wipe out every single American, or Asian, or African. Now *that* is abnormal. Killing off entire factions because of their dissimilarities is like burning down a neighborhood because the houses don't match.

It couldn't possibly be true that wholesale massacres are wired into humanity's DNA, and so it must be learned. Those who think genocide is acceptable have been influenced by their own culture, or by other circumstances. Fortunately there's a cure for that. With adequate information and life experience, ethics are bound to kick in.

Ethics and morality are established by cultures and religions and nations, but I'm a firm believer in gut instincts.[89] Your upbringing etches a lot of ideas in granite, but we humans are more malleable than stone. We have an inherent capacity to think for ourselves, and we must let our conscience be our guide.

I know it can be hard to step outside the ideals that have been pounded into our minds and injected into our marrow. It takes courage to differ. It's even more difficult if the popular view is global, like amassing as much money as one can lay hands on.

Humans are assigned "worth" by the global society, and as capitalism is the most successfully panoramic "ism" humans have ever known, worth is based on finances. Gah! There are so many other ways to gauge the worth of a being!

Talk show hosts have given away lots of money and possessions in response to driving desire, but it seems misplaced. Ellen DeGeneres once gifted a woman who appeared resistant to owning possessions of any kind, but the gift was given as an act of kindness. Which is worth more? Silly question.

Money might or might not buy love, freedom, and the other concepts we value most. But it cannot be a measure of a human being's worth. It would be like saying animals and trees have no value unless they generate an income for someone. Ridiculous.

---

89 Ya think? This entire series is about common sense, a phenomenon that often manifests as a visceral burbling in the gut.

R.L. George

Another potential for absurdity is superstitions, but then again, not so much. Supernatural phenomena and the superstitions they create are laughed at by our current scientific society, but great thinkers of the past have had to dodge chuckles and cynicism until their ideas could be proved. Dismissing everything that can't be proved is taking cynicism to a dangerous edge.

Extremes aside, stepping around ladders and dodging the paths of black cats are harmless activities. Until we know what drives superstitious behaviors, there's no reason to studiously avoid them.

An example is a sports star who refuses to allow a certain grass stain to be washed out of his uniform. He continues to excel as long as that stain is there. In some scientist's reality, it's because he has wired his own brain to that stain, and he's excelling on his own merits, but who cares? Cultures that thrived for thousands of years used the same type of techniques, and they thrived, right? It doesn't matter that they didn't know the source of their luck, or skill.

I say all of that because it will be thousands of years—if ever—before we know the absolute science of everything that ever was and ever will be. Shall we plod along with hesitation until we've got all the facts? No need. Superstitions are intuitively guiding us, so let us have them. No need to harass people who scour sidewalks for cracks to avoid and heads-up pennies to grab.

Mean teasing and mocking others breaks my heart. I thrive on goodwill and friendship. There's a very strong possibility that we're all deeply interconnected, and everything we do reverberates through time and space. I'd rather vibrate positive energy.

Harsh words thrown toward a passing stranger could impact others. How could that be? Easy. That stranger goes

Myth of Normal

home and spreads his bad mood to his family, who go on to bring it into their schools and workplaces, and on it goes like a virus. It's like the wannabe-race car driver who leaves nervous wrecks in his wake without seeing it, because he continues to blithely speed along.

We all leave a wake behind us, or we cause ripples from our splash, and as luck would have it, the same can happen with acts of caring.

I suspect many people have stories of how a single kindness has spread outward. My most recent was when I was waiting for a doctor's appointment. Through the windows to the outside I saw a woman pushing a man in a wheelchair toward the door, and I went to open it for them. While I waited about ten more minutes for my doctor, I saw other patients standing to open doors for those who were sicker, and I witnessed it once more after my appointment was finished. The energy in the big waiting room had become lighter, despite it being a doctor's office.

Did I inspire others or had I been subconsciously inspired by someone else that day? No matter. The connections we make while out in public have their impacts, and I prefer that it helps rather than hurts.

Admittedly, there have been times when I felt mad at the world, and it's likely I spread that around, too. Apologies if the waves of those behaviors ever rolled over you.

We all have our quirks, but we don't always recognize them as such. Worse, we can wildly resist owning up to flawed thoughts or actions after they've been brought to our attention. It takes a brave and witty realist to say, with authentic regret, "Oops, my bad."

Once we've gained enough wisdom, we learn to avoid assumptions and presumptions. It's imprudent to assume that you will never be wrong, just as it's pitiful to think you can never be right.

In that line of reasoning, it's also shameful to suppose a poor person is worthless, or a different race is inferior, or a young person is automatically rebellious. One never really knows until the individual is known. That's the key to overcoming a fear of not knowing what's what. Enter every new interaction with the understanding that knee-jerk judgments hit people below the belt. First, learn who people are, and bear in mind that you'd like them to do the same for you.

While you're learning to respect others, you're teaching yourself to honor your own fine self.

We humans are social creatures, but we're all alone inside our minds. Getting along with yourself helps you to get along with all the other social creatures wandering the planet. I'm advocating geniality, though, not conformity.

Attempting to conform can strip one of thinking for oneself. It can literally kill, and I use the word "literally" in its literal sense. One example can be found in stories about the atrocities of war, where soldiers use the chilling, free-pass statement, "I was only following orders." Throughout this book, I've been beseeching people to resist conformity.

Imagine that everyone in the world was crazy except for you. You, as the only sane person, would be abnormal. Would you conform and try to stir up some insanity within yourself? Join 'em because the numbers were against you?

Now that I think that through, I'm not sure of how I myself would respond. There are too many variables, like how would one recognize insanity, as such, if it were the norm. The best way I can put it is no matter how much everyone wanted me to join in on crazy behaviors, I would likely resist. I know this because it's something I try to do here, in our current kooky world.

Myth of Normal

We don't need to measure our mental and emotional capacity against that of others. It doesn't take much to tap into common sense about safety when a group of friends wants to have a drinking contest, or worse, a drinking and driving contest. Our own perspective of rationality should top that of a hundred people who want to go on a looting rampage after a local catastrophe.

Among the countries and cultures in the world, mental health is subjective. Some American traditions appear downright dysfunctional to those in other nations, and we can look at commonplace practices of others as deranged. (As a reminder, one culture drops babies from a 50 temple. They don't see anything wrong with that.)

The best we can do is exercise our minds and hope that we can learn and think capably. I'm not talking about smart versus unintelligent, I'm referring to allowing our sponge-like brains to do their thing, which is soaking up knowledge. Once we have a firm grip on knowledge, we have a better chance of understanding the world around us. It's a big world, so it requires a lot of patience, but it's worth it because getting a grip on the ins and outs of lunacy can help to reduce stress.

Well, for the most part. For instance, it can be stressful to understand why a war is coming, and why there's nothing a regular citizen can do to stop it. Or, it's understandable that regular citizens are told by their governments to temper their private habits, like smoking or drinking, yet so many people are reluctant to modify those lifestyles.

It's politically incorrect to suggest that smokers and drinkers ought to be left to themselves, let them do their thing, don't make laws against them. There I went and said it anyway. I've heard that attitude called everything from "natural selection" to "freedom."

I'm a believer of allowing individuals to make their own

mistakes, as long as they aren't hurting others. Yes, second-hand smoke can be harmful but smokers are regulated to dark corners of the street and sealed rooms in airports. Automobile emissions are a thousand times more harmful than second-hand smoke, but our world is taking their time fixing that one.

Electric vehicles were first conceived and built in the !!1800s!! and have been available ever since. Somebody[90] preferred gas-power, and so we're only now trying to transfer over to electric. Why was the poisoning of planet Earth ignored for so long? It wasn't politically correct until now.

Hopefully, the children of the future will have cleaner air and clearer horizons.

Children are, and always have been, quite fascinating human beings, with their curiosity and potential. Parents who wish for their kids to fit in may find the opposite occurs, and parents who want their children to become abnormally rich, famous, and/or powerful are often let down. All we can do is teach them by modeling the behaviors we hope they'll adopt.

Modeling is the best way to teach, in my opinion. Telling someone to think a certain way or to behave as instructed isn't very effective. Even worse is to enter a conversation with expectations about how the other(s) should respond. We've all done it, we write a script in our minds, and then we're surprised when the other(s) drop or mess up their lines. What to do?

Rely on natural discourse. Agree, disagree, move forward, move on. When we assume directorship over interactions we're gambling with failure. Failure can be all at once depressing and aggravating. Who needs it? Trust that those who are speaking have something to say. Listen. The potential for understanding increases exponentially.

---

90 Full name: Somebody O.I.L. Barons

Myth of Normal

A creative way to approach interacting with others is to look at them as founts of information. Their words speak encyclopedic volumes, and their actions are entire libraries of input about who they are. Staying open to creative perspectives is of utmost importance, and that goes beyond socializing.

Creativity reaches far and wide, it goes over and under and around every walk of life. It's a part of every discipline, including all of the sciences. There are elements of creativity in evolution and in the history of civilization. It can inform and entertain, it can be therapeutic in relationships and lifesaving in emergencies. The capacity for human beings to be creative is as important as the stuff of life because it's the stuff of living.

Creative artists are notoriously abnormal, and proud of it. Stories of mentally ill creative artists abound, but I think that's overplayed. We hear the most about people who make a splash. Otherwise, artists are about as psychologically sound as any given person shopping around the great mall of their society.

That might be a case of "damned by faint praise." As I've often asked in these pages, who really knows how to set a general standard of sanity, much less normality? Psychologists, I suppose, but it's not a given that they're the most sane characters in the play.

Psychology's definition of normal is nebulous, at best. Even as it's defined it groups people into being average if they're an overweight American, or nervous when they're the new face at a party. Then, the therapists lean forward in their armchairs and say, "How can ve zolve your problem?"

I'm not a therapist[91] but I have studied psychology at

---

91 Although like most, I do engage in friend therapy

great length, and I still rely on common sense more often than some textbook assertion about how to deal with discomfort. Psychology textbooks and scientific studies are seeking generalized answers, but just my luck, the generalizations don't apply to me. My intuition tells me to therefore trust my own gut.

One of the reasons social anxiety is surprisingly common is because we all know there are norms that don't fit us. We are not all alike, but there's that inescapable expectation of conformity. At one party stands a wallflower who's distressed by all the excessive drinking, and is anxious to start saying goodbyes for the night. At another party is a wallflower watching everyone converse without a sip of beer, wine, or spirits, and can't wait to slip away.

I don't mean my examples to be seen as a teetotaler and an alcoholic. I'm focusing on anyman or anywoman who can be described as a social drinker, but happens to be uncomfortable in a particular setting. In both scenarios, a deeper look at the "wallflower" position will reveal that social anxiety is the biggest contributor to the discomfort.

Here's where my own suggestion comes in. If you're determined to get out of the house and go to a party, add texture to your self-pep-talk. If it has to do with alcohol, tell yourself people are bound to drink, and maybe you can have fun observing the degrees of change in personalities after an hour. Or, if you're the second person at the other party, have a glass of wine before you arrive, and then focus on the intriguing feel of everyone else who's enjoying substance-free energy.

Those suggestions are meant to be an illustration of a broader concept. Social anxiety can rise up at a party or a restaurant, a softball game or a grocery store. It isn't the drinking or eating, the cheers at a game, or the unabashed yacking of people checking product choices on cellphone calls with spouses.

The anxiety is related to wondering if we fit in, and the best I can suggest is to rewrite your inner dialogue. Remind yourself that no two grains of sand are alike, and the same is true of snowflakes, and the same is true of partiers, diners, athletes, and shoppers.

I don't fit in with everyone else, and even among my friends and family our differences are vast. Family is actually a good example of the ridiculous notion that people can be normal or average. I've known countless individuals who were born and raised by the same parents, in the same neighborhood, in the same era, and are nothing alike. I don't know any siblings who are like peas in a pod, to use that worn out expression.

Come to think of it, another relevant expression is "fits like a glove," but ironically, that implies two totally separate things. One is the human hand, which is so amazing that it has built everything except nature itself. The other is a useful item that will warm or protect the amazing hand. The importance of the hand versus the glove is a no-brainer, and yet "fits like a glove" is a classic example of symbiotic a relationship.

I don't mean to imply that one should see oneself as either a hand or a glove. My thoughts are around relationships that can flourish despite differences. That's one of my philosophies, and it's similar to philosophies that have been developed over eons.

Fitting in with others is never a given. Sure, someone can find a book club or a church or a bar where everyone knows their name, but the closer you get to others, the more your differences will start to glow. The trick is to accept loving relationships as the glue that will hold us together despite the fact that none of us is quite like the other.

The common sense concept that we must think for

ourselves is powerful. Input from others is fabulous, but when we simply *follow* other leads of thought, we're stripped of our uniqueness. Our freedom of decision is drained away. Making an effort to be normal is wasting valuable you-time.

Normality is a myth that's no different than anything found in Aesop's Fables. There is a moral to the story of normality, which is that individuals must find common ground in order to merge into societies. What I try to do is dive off the cliff of normal morality and explore deep, hidden caverns.

The most profound moral of the myth of normal is its counterexample. The best way to grasp the concept of "average" is to recognize its nefarious implications, like how buying into conformity comes at the cost of your private mind. Once that comes clear, it's easier to be brave and wise enough stand out as distinct among so many billions of humans.

There is a slanted side (as opposed to a downside) to becoming fully independent, to being utterly autonomous in the celebration of our uniqueness. After all I've said here, I must remind myself of all the ways we're alike, just not alike in the ways we'd expect. Breathing, sentient beings? Yes. Do human bodies have the same basic characteristics? Sure. Do we all have the same beliefs, politics, qualities and flaws, do we have the same sense of humor and identical measures of decorum? Of course not.

Honoring your sense of self, and respecting all the ingredients of you, gives you the power to honor and respect everyone else who's struggling through this outrageous experience we call life.

Trust yourself and you may set standards, rather than follow them. This is not to say we can avoid following *all* standards, and in fact, we're expected to behave as lawful citizens. That is the only condition under which it's a great idea to stick with normality. Yes. Freedom is best maintained when we follow our society's proscribed rules of legal conduct, at least as often as that's possible, but embracing your abnormal self is the most freeing feeling of all.

R.L. George

MISFIT

Note: The laws cited in this story are actual laws. You can't make this stuff up.

I didn't do it.

I've been accused of breaking federal laws, and of course if that's true I should go to prison. The prison would not have a golf course or its own Netflix series. It would be exactly what I've imagined to be "hard time." Chipping away at a megalithic stone with a tiny rock hammer, slurping buggy swill for meals, etching scratches in my cell wall to count the days, months, years.

Alright, I admit it, I don't really know if that's how it would be. It doesn't matter because I'm innocent. I'm innocently doing my life, that's all, and I don't think it's my fault that some of my behaviors are considered illegal.

When the FBI first knocked on my door I invited them in, and as I closed the door they checked out my place by looking upwards, the way people do in old-timey TV shows. They were a boy and a girl, both wearing Men in Black suits without the sunglasses, which would have been pushing the point on that dark-clouded day.

I'll call them Nietzsche and Rand. I choose Nietzsche for the boy because he (the original Nietzsche) had a way of slapping out aphorisms, like "What does not kill me, makes me stronger." Does the FBI kill people? If they don't, does it make people stronger?

Agent Nietzsche said, "You need to talk to us." He smiled a bit when he said it, but it sounded even more threatening than the odious, "We need to talk."

I'm calling the woman Rand because Ayn Rand wrote books with characters who were cemented in their ideals, determined to either fight or abandon those who disagreed with them. There's also some irony that Rand the writer was a Russian immigrant, and the female FBI agent had a Russian-sounding name that was so long and unpronounceable, I've chosen to replace it with a single syllable. The formidable Agent Rand.

We sat together in my living room and Agent Nietzsche asked, "Do you know it's against the law to lie to the FBI?"

"No!" I blurted out, and then slapped my hands over my mouth. My blurting problem, that's one of those regrettable elements of my life. However, there's a difference between a crime and a nervous accident. Yes, I did know about criminal lying, and I'm usually much better at presenting a poker face, but there I went lying and busting my own self in the space of two seconds. In truth (I mean that honestly), a part of my brain first heard the question as, "Did you break the law?"

When Agent Rand spoke, her eyes darted around my living room like a detective, once again acting like someone from one of those old black-and-white TV shows. She recited the "Don't lie to the FBI" code as if quoting scripture, and then the interview began in earnest.

"Tell us about your background," Agent Nietzsche commanded.

Oh, no. I have to talk about my background without dissembling, prevaricating, or lying by omission? I stallingly offered them coffee but they both refused. Agent Rand took a water bottle from behind her back, apparently retrieving it from some sort of spy-issue fanny-pack hidden on her buttock.

"I have to admit—" bad start, restart: "I should warn you that I've been a misfit since I was a kid, throughout my teens, and during my entire adulthood."

"We don't need to go all the way back."

"That's a relief. I did make an effort to fit in, you know, to do what everyone else does. Like, once when I was about thirteen I tried to steal a candy bar, but I failed to close the deal. It was at a Fast-Mart, and there were two people at the registers. I took a wide, flat candy bar, stuck it down the front of my pants, and strolled to the checkout counter. The cashiers were a boy and a girl, just like you two."

My interlocutors exchanged a glance, each raising their right eyebrows, giving them an opposite-mirror effect.

"But younger," I stumbled along. "Not that you're oldsters. They were just teenagers. Mind if I make some coffee for myself?"

We relocated to the kitchen, the agents sat at the table, and I muttered small talk while I filled the kettle. "So, I'm standing at the counter ordering a frozen cola, reaching into my pocket for some change, and the candy bar slips down my leg and lands on the floor. I peered into the eyes of both cashiers to see if they heard it, and they both seemed to think I was flirting. The boy turned to the frozen cola machine and the girl walked out from behind the counter to fix a gum display. I stepped on the candy bar at my feet to hide it." I was babbling. "I stood there for half an hour while customers came and went, until finally both cashiers were back behind the counter and I could dash away. I formally apologize for attempting to steal a candy bar, and I believe I've served ample time by castigating myself throughout the following decades."

"What we need," said Agent Nietzsche, "is background information relevant to the crimes you have committed."

"Allegedly!" was shouted, but not by me. Agent Rand knew the rules.

The kettle shrilly whistled. "I know what you're

wondering," I said, once again breaking the law by lying to the FBI. "You want to know why I have a potbellied pig." I stirred some cream into my coffee and joined the agents at the table. "That's because people don't generally eat potbellied pigs."

It gave me a little glee that they couldn't object to this new topic. Agent Rand sipped from her bottle of water, while Agent Nietzsche folded a stick of gum into his mouth.

While Nietzsche chewed Rand informed me that my pet pig had caused me to violate Title 18, USC section 1857. "It's a federal crime to allow your pig to enter a fenced area on public land. It might damage the grass. Ownership of a potbellied pig is not a question or a problem, it's the pig's actions that are of concern."

I sat at the table with my coffee. "Listen, Zephyr is a good pig."

"Zephyr?" asked Rand.

"He's fast, sometimes like the wind."

Neither of them wrote down the name of my pig, but surely they were recording my conversation. Anyone who could hide a bottle of water behind her back, hands-free, must have a few more tricks in her garter belt. "Did Zephyr get away from you?" Rand asked. "You have to *knowingly* allow the pig access to the fenced-in area."

"Yeah," I said, in an accidental mobster accent, "that's it! He dashed away and next thing I knew, he was hauling shank around the grass. I didn't allow him to do it, he just took off, squealing like..."

Agent Nietzsche had masticated his gum into submission, and now he said, "You allowed him to squeal? You were in a national park. That's a violation of Title 18 USC section 1865 and Title 36, C.F.R. section 2.15(a)(4)."

Could anybody have said anything other than, "Huh?"

Agent Rand explained. "It's a federal crime to let your pig, or any pet, make noises that will scare the wildlife."

I repeated my monosyllabic sound of confusion.

Nietzsche said, "You were breaking another law."

"What about the 'knowingly' part?"

"You didn't hear Zephyr squealing?"

I cupped my hand behind my ear and said, "Say what?" but they didn't care for the pun.

Agent Rand adopted a reasonable tone. "Animals can be hard to control. However, your own actions are of greater concern, here."

This is where things got sticky. Although I'd had no idea about breaking any laws at the time I committed them, the park ranger had indeed spelled each of them out to me as I broke them. I'll call the park ranger Genghis for reasons I shouldn't have to explain.

"My actions," I said, "were *re*actions. The ranger screamed at me – isn't there a law against that?"

"According to the ranger, he was using a firm, clear tone to cite the reasons that he was reporting you for arrest."

"It sounded like he was screaming them at me."

Nietzsche interjected his opinion: "He may have been attempting to make himself heard over the squealing Zephyr."

It seemed like a good time to laugh, but I couldn't even dredge up a smile. "It was all a misunderstanding."

"Did you try to bribe a national park ranger?"

"No! I tried to make up for Zephyr's misbehavior by offering the ranger some snacks. He refused, and accused me of offering him a bribe. I said, 'Then just give me a buck so that you're buying these goodies from me, and then it wouldn't be a bribe.'"

Nietzsche raised a finger. "But that's when you broke another law."

"He told me as much, but I didn't believe him." When Genghis finished his ranting about Zephyr's criminal behaviors—which I subsequently learned were based on real, honest-to-weirdness laws—I had offered him the remainder of my picnic. That was when he insisted that he wasn't someone who could be bribed, and so I suggested he give me a buck for the goodies. As far as I was concerned, there was no bribing whatsoever going on in his forest.

Genghis had chosen that moment to start a new rant, referring to my offer of packaged, preservative-saturated, frozen onion rings. I'd been planning to use a camper's food-warmer to cook them, but I'd had a change of appetite after taking a closer look at the ingredients. I may have been hungry, but those things appeared to have actual poison in them. (Hence the offer to Genghis, but I wasn't about to admit to anything nobody had accused me of doing.)

I said to the agents, present-time, "How was I supposed to know he wasn't a fan of onion rings?"

"His preferences are irrelevant," Agent Rand reasoned. "Title 21, USC section 333, and 21 CFR section 102.39 describe the crime of selling onion rings that look like regular onion rings when in fact they're made from diced onion."

"He wasn't kidding about that?"

Nietzsche volunteered, "It's the law."

"And then," Rand added, "there was the wine."

"He wasn't making that up? I mean, what he said about the wine?"

"He wasn't making that up," Nietzsche stated. "According to Title 27 USC section 207, section 205(e) and 27 C.F.R. section 4.39(a)(9) it's a federal crime to sell wine that has the word 'zombie' in its brand name."

I waited for the agents to start giggling, and to tell me they were just messin' with my head. They sat there with their

FBI faces, neutral (but not quite zombie-like) expressions, awaiting my reply. What could I say? "'Zombie' is not part of the brand name of that wine. It did have pictures of zombies on the label, though. And there was a big white spot on the label where I could write in the word."

"Why did you write in the word?" asked Nietzsche, but Rand interrupted him with a compliment, "Your writing was an excellent copy of the other writing on the label."

I responded to Nietzsche. "I had a single glass and it was very strong. I sat there looking at the picture on the label, thinking, 'This could knock me into my grave. Would I want to come back as a zombie?' I had my pencil with me, and thought it would be fun to add the word." I nodded to Rand. "I did my best to make it look real. It wasn't anything but something to do."

"Well," she said, "by telling the park ranger that it would give him, quote, 'a great buzz for a buck,' you were breaking another law."

"Okay, really?"

"Really. Title 27, USC section 205, 207 and 27 CFR section 4.64(a)(8). It's a federal crime to suggests that wine has intoxicating qualities."

"What wine doesn't have intoxicating qualities?"

"There's non-alcoholic wine," noted Nietzsche.

"You mean grape juice?"

"This is not a laughing matter."

"Grape juice doesn't make me laugh anywhere near as much as wine does."

The agents' expressions lost their neutral quality.

"Listen," I said. "Park Ranger Khan *hit* me. He shoved my shoulder with a smack of his hand. Isn't assault against the law anymore?"

Rand said, "Park Ranger Khan" (that really was his last

name, I guess I could have explained that earlier), "was within his rights to hit you."

"No way."

"Way." Nietzsche had apparently reverted to a K-6 playground, but then he got back to business. "You were exceptionally annoying. Title 7 USC section 1011(f) and 36 CFR section 261.4(b) makes it criminal to say something so annoying in a national forest that a person hits you."

"You mean I could have hit *him*? Legally?"

Ha! That got a "Huh?" out of him.

"The things he had been saying were annoying *me*."

"But – "

"And why is it annoying to call a flashlight a torch?"

"Reportedly, it's the way you said it," said Rand, "combined with the fact that you had broken yet another law by damaging his flashlight."

I said, "I don't understand," which was understandable.

"According to Title 40, USC section 8103(b)(4) it's a federal crime to hurt a government-owned lamp."

"Well, as much as that may be true—I'm going to have to trust you on that—when Ranger Khan told my about that law, I pointed out that a flashlight isn't a lamp. It's a flashlight. I mentioned that in England they call it a torch. Flashlights and torches are not the same as lamps. And by the way, when I tossed the onion rings to Zephyr, who bumped the ranger's flashlight, *Khan* is the one who dropped it into the firepit. All I did was explain the definition of 'lamp' to him."

Rand asked me, "Did you raise your voice when you offered those details?"

"No."

"Were you condescending?"

"If I were the condescending type, wouldn't I have started sounding that way by now?" In retrospect, this might not have been the most soothing suggestion. I added, "Am I the only one who thinks these rules and regulations are pretty wild?" That seemed to work.

"I imagine," said Rand, "that you might have used a tone of insult while speaking with Ranger Khan. However, we can give you some leeway. Because the laws you had broken are a bit... obscure, you might have been thinking that the ranger had been inventing one or more of them."

That's when I noticed the tingle of a smile on Agent Rand's face. Agent Nietzsche's expression had returned to its static blandness, but his eyes had picked up a flicker of amusement.

When I next spoke, it was with awed respect. "You *do* think these laws are ridiculous!"

"We know the law," came her only reply. Was she correcting me, implying that she didn't *think* the laws were ridiculous, but *knew* it?

Agent Nietzsche pushed back from the kitchen table but his hands rested there a moment longer. "You have a spotless record. We're letting you off with a warning, but you and your pig are banned from national parks for one year." He stood and extended his hand, and I stood to shake it, still awed.

Agent Rand reached over to shake my hand, too. I asked her, "How do you memorize all the details of those laws?"

"You're not the only interview we have scheduled today. You'd be amazed by how often this sort of thing happens."

As they walked out my door, Agent Nietzsche tossed a few final words over his shoulder. "This kind of nutty stuff is normal."

End

Made in the USA
Las Vegas, NV
22 January 2023

66062307R00132